Postindustrial Germany

Published in our
centenary year
～ **2004** ～
MANCHESTER
UNIVERSITY
PRESS

ISSUES IN GERMAN POLITICS

Edited by
Professor Charlie Jeffery, Institute for German Studies
Dr Charles Lees, University of Sussex

Issues in German Politics is a major new series on contemporary Germany. Focusing on the post-unity era, it presents concise, scholarly analyses of the forces driving change in domestic politics and foreign policy. Key themes will be the continuing legacies of German unification and controversies surrounding Germany's role and power in Europe. The series includes contributions from political science, international relations and political economy.

Already published:

Bulmer, Jeffery and Paterson: *Germany's European diplomacy: Shaping the regional milieu*

Green: *The politics of exclusion: Institutions and immigration policy in contemporary Germany*

Gunlicks: *The* Länder *and German federalism*

Harding and Paterson (eds): *The future of the German economy: An end to the miracle?*

Harnisch and Maull: *Germany as a Civilian Power? The foreign policy of the Berlin Republic*

Hyde-Price: *Germany and European order: Enlarging NATO and the EU*

Lees: *The Red–Green coalition in Germany: Politics, personalities and power*

Rittberger (ed.): *German foreign policy since unification: Theories and case studies*

Postindustrial Germany

Services, technological transformation and knowledge in unified Germany

Claire Annesley

Manchester University Press

Manchester and New York

Distributed exclusively in the USA by Palgrave

Published by Manchester University Press
Oxford Road, Manchester M13 9NR, UK
and Room 400, 175 Fifth Avenue, New York, NY 10010, USA
www.manchesteruniversitypress.co.uk

Distributed exclusively in the USA by
Palgrave, 175 Fifth Avenue, New York,
NY 10010, USA

Distributed exclusively in Canada by
UBC Press, University of British Columbia, 2029 West Mall,
Vancouver, BC, Canada V6T 1Z2

British Library Cataloguing-in-Publication Data
A catalogue record for this book is available from the British Library

Library of Congress Cataloging-in-Publication Data applied for

ISBN 0 7190 6536 4 *hardback*

First published 2004

13 12 11 10 09 08 07 06 05 04   10 9 8 7 6 5 4 3 2 1

Typeset in Minion
by Northern Phototypesetting Co. Ltd, Bolton
Printed in Great Britain
by Bell & Bain Ltd, Glasgow

To Sascha, with love

Contents

List of tables

Acknowledgements

Postindustrial Germany is very much a moving target. While it has been a challenge to keep up with events in contemporary Germany, I have been fortunate to have the support of the best institutions, colleagues and friends. At the risk of gushing, I would like to thank them all here.

At Sheffield University, the Germanic Studies Department and the Political Economy Research Centre (PERC) were the most stimulating and friendly places imaginable. I would particularly like thank my friends and colleagues Andrew Gamble, Gavin Kelly, Mike Kenny, Steve Ludlam, Sylvia McColm, Moray McGowan, Tony Payne, Jonathan Perraton, Maurice Roche, Peter Thompson, Peter Wells and Karl Wilds for their support and encouragement.

Fortunately the Government Department at Manchester University has matched Sheffield's qualities on almost all counts – unfortunately it is just not located on the sunny side of the Pennines. I am eternally grateful to the Government Department for appointing me in 2000 and to Simon Bulmer, David Farrell, Norman Geras, Yoram Gorlizki, Jill Lovecy, Geoff Roberts, Ursula Vogel and Rorden Wilkinson for their support and kindness since I arrived. I would also like to thank the Department for allowing me to go on sabbatical in 2002/3. This gave me the perfect opportunity to spend some time in Germany to update the material for this book. During my research leave I benefited enormously from the support of a German Academic Exchange Service (DAAD) scholarship (award ref. A/02/23751) and then a British Academy Grant (award ref. SG-34687). I would like to thank Professor Jürgen Kocka and Professor Günter Schmid of the *Wissenschaftszentrum zu Berlin* (WZB) for their hospitality during the months I spent at their institution.

The staff at Manchester University Press and the comments of an anonymous reviewer were most helpful in the final stages of preparing this manuscript. But the fact that this book was ever finished has to do with the continual support, love and care of my family – Mum, Johnny, Dad and big sister Karen – and my three additional 'families' in Dublin, Nottingham and Grünberg. Thank you so very much to my best friend Gillian Pye, Sadie and Graham Ovenden and to Lucy and Eve James and Nick Stevenson. A final thank you goes to my partner Sascha Feuchert. I just cannot imagine how the last few years would have been without his faith, love and humour. This book is dedicated to him.

List of abbreviations

ABM   *Arbeitsbeschaffungsmassnahmen*
BetrVG Betriebsverfassungsgesetz (Works Constitutions Act)
CDU   Christlich Demokratische Union (Christian Democratic
            Union)
CHE   Centrum für Hochschulentwicklung (Centre for the
            Development of Higher Education)
DAG   Deutsche Angestelltengewerkschaft (German Union of Salaried
            Employees)
DGB   Deutscher Gewerkschaftsbund (German Trade Union
            Federation)
DPG   Deutsche Postgewerkschaft (German Postal Workers Union)
EU   European Union
FDGB   Freier Deutscher Gewerkschaftsbund (Free German Trade
            Union Federation)
FDP   Freie Demokratische Partei (Free Democratic Party)
FRG   Federal Republic of Germany
GDP   gross domestic product
GDR   German Democratic Republic
hbv   Gewerkschaft Handel, Banken und Versicherung (Commerce,
            Banking and Insurance Union)
ILO   International Labour Organisation
IT   information technology
ITR   Information Technology Revolution
OECD   Organisation for Economic Co-operation and Development
ÖTV   Gewerkschaft Öffentliche Dienste, Transport und Verkehr
            (Union for Public Service, Transport and Communication)
PDS   Partei des Demokratischen Sozialismus
PERC   Political Economy Research Centre

PISA	Programme for International Student Assessment
PSA	PersonalServiceAgentur (Personnel Service Agency)
SED	Sozialistische Einheitspartei (Socialist Unity Party)
SME	small and medium-sized enterprise
SPD	Sozialdemokratische Partei Deutschlands (Social Democratic Party of Germany)
ver.di	Vereinte Dienstleistungsgewerkschaft (Unified Service Sector Union)
VW	Volkswagen

Introduction

The German model of capitalism has acquired a bad reputation in recent years. From a number of different perspectives it has been argued that this co-ordinated and consensual way of organising capitalism is no longer competitive in the modern economic environment. For example, many globalisation theories proposed that social market and consensus based economic models will inevitably have to converge with liberal market economies (Held *et al.* 1999). The end of history theorists have claimed that since the collapse of the socialist alternative, there is only one way to organise capitalist economies, and that is in the liberal market way (Fukuyama 1992). A further, but less explored, area of research assesses Germany's transition to a postindustrial economy and society and characterises it as underdeveloped or backward. Germany has remained, it is argued, 'resolutely industrial' (Lash and Urry 1994) and has struggled to expand service sector employment (Manow and Seils 2000). Moreover, Germany prides itself on being a country that promotes high standards of education and training, and yet it has shown signs of weakness in the transition to the knowledge economy (Doherty 1997). It has even introduced a controversial green card scheme to meet the demand for highly skilled information technology (IT) specialists. Yet on the other hand, a number of studies have demonstrated Germany's strength in adapting existing industrial technologies to the new economic paradigm (Herrigel 1996; Soskice 1999) and have pointed to the innovative potential of some parts of eastern Germany (Bowley 1998; Norten-Standen 1997).

This book looks at Germany's transition to a postindustrial state. It challenges the idea that Germany is lagging behind in the process of postindustrial transition on account of its notoriously underdeveloped service sector, and assesses instead Germany's performance across three contrasting approaches to postindustrial economy and society. To do this

the book breaks down the concept of the postindustrial economy and
society into three elements: the service sector, technological transformation and the knowledge economy. It then demonstrates how unified Germany is transforming and performing according to each of these criteria
of postindustrialism.

Postindustrial Germany argues that national models of industrial capitalism develop along different postindustrial trajectories in a path-dependent
way. What is more, regionally differentiated postindustrial transitions
emerge within nation states. *Postindustrial Germany* rejects generalisations
about the current resolutely industrial nature of the German model and
demonstrates instead the complex and nuanced postindustrial structure of
unified Germany.

Chapter 1 sets the scene for this study. It outlines what is meant by the
German model of capitalism and how it has been performing in recent
years. It contrasts the debates between those who believe that distinctive
models of capitalism will converge to a single paradigm and those who
argue that capitalist models will remain distinct. While siding with institutionalist positions which argue that difference will persist, it highlights
some of the limitations inherent in institutionalist defences of the German
model. It is argued that these either ignore the fact that Germany is
an internally diverse economy or they fail to deal with Germany as a
dynamic political economy which is responding to the challenges of the
postindustrial transformation.

Chapter 2 offers a broad outline of the concept of the postindustrial
economy and society. First it contrasts three ways of conceptualising the
postindustrial political economy: as a shift from a manufacturing to a
service sector economy (Bell 1974; Esping-Andersen 1990); as the transformation of systems of production from mass production to flexible
specialisation as a consequence of technological developments (Amin
1994; Castells 1996; Sabel 1994; 1995; Soskice 1999); and the concept of
the knowledge economy (Berger 1996; Hodgson 1999). Then it weighs up
the arguments between those who assert that the postindustrial transformation will result in a convergence of capitalist economies to a single
model and those who believe that institutions embedded at the national
level will shape the outcomes of the postindustrial state. Chapter 2 proposes an inclusive version of postindustrial transition that recognises that
all of these kinds of transition are taking place within Germany: there is
an increase in service sector activity, there is transformation of national
production systems and there is an increase in the significance of knowledge. Moreover, it is argued that there is no single uniform model of the

postindustrial economy. Instead it proposes that this is a differentiated process which is clearly shaped by the formal and informal institutions which exist at national and regional levels. This framework is adopted in Chapters 3, 4 and 5 to analyse the dimensions of the postindustrial economy of contemporary Germany.

In Chapter 3 the nature of service sector development in Germany is analysed in detail. In much recent analysis the slow growth of Germany's service sector is frequently cited as the source of its economic difficulties (Manow and Seils 2000). According to this view, the key to rejuvenating Germany's economy lies in the deregulation of the labour market and an expansion of service sector economic activity. This chapter deals with the German relationship with the service sector, highlighting the fact that in Germany there has been a reluctance to develop this area because of the cultural importance of industrial employment in Germany, because of the bad reputation that service sector employment has – it is associated with the Anglo-American society of haves and have-nots (Häußermann and Siebel 1995) – and also because of the fact that the provision of many caring services has been carried out by unpaid females in the context of the family. The chapter argues that service sector activity has been under-reported in Germany as much is hidden in the manufacturing sector (Castells 1996). Moreover it proposes that in deindustrialised, eastern Germany, where there is still high unemployment, the attitude towards service employment is more positive and there has been a rapid growth of this kind of employment. The chapter closes by outlining some key developments in the expansion of the service sector postindustrial trajectories in unified Germany, highlighting how formal and informal institutions affect this development in different regions. It looks at recent attempts to expand the service economy, at measures to encourage women into employment and at the regulation of the service sector though the establishment of a large trade union for workers in this sector.

Chapter 4 deals with technological transformation as an indicator of postindustrialism. It is concerned with the capacity of national models of capitalism and their respective industrial production systems to adjust to the new global markets and the new post-Fordist or flexible specialisation production methods (Amin 1994; Piore and Sabel 1984). In contrast to the literature on the service sector economy, here Germany is portrayed as being quite advanced in this kind of postindustrial transition (Soskice 1999), and certain regions, such as the south-west are highlighted as being particularly exemplary (Sabel 1994; Herrigel 1996). It is argued that, using the indicator of technological transition, Germany is better placed as a postindustrial economy than a number of its competitors. This has to do with institutions – such as innovation systems and works councils – which promote gradual and incremental technological transitions. The chapter also highlights the limits of this analysis by arguing that the positive effect of these institutions seems to be running out in the west and that this analysis is clearly restricted to western Germany and does not account for the east. Despite the fact that the institutions of the German model were transferred to the east at the time of unification, there is little evidence that the same virtuous effect exists in the east. Instead, the east was deindustrialised and there are no industrial production systems to transform, though some new technologies are being introduced directly from scratch. Some of the potentially most dynamic technological regions are springing up in eastern Germany (Bowley 1998). The chapter finally looks at some recent developments in institutions of the German model which support technological transition.

Chapter 5 looks in more detail at the third version of the postindustrial economy and society, in which knowledge is considered the most important commodity and factor of production driving innovation and economic growth (Hodgson 1999). This chapter considers the role of knowledge in the German model and argues that, in Germany, knowledge and skills have always been highly regarded and this is reflected in the highly-skilled workforce and strong innovation and training systems which persist into the current era (Harding and Soskice 2000). As such, Germany has a competitive advantage in that its knowledge systems are well entrenched institutionally. However, it is becoming apparent that the institutionalised systems are good at producing and reproducing certain kinds of knowledge but bad at developing others. For example, the German education system performed badly in the recent Organisation for Economic Co-operation and Development (OECD) Programme for International Student Assessment (PISA) study and this triggered discussions about how to reform the education and training system to make it more responsive to the demands of the contemporary economy. Germany has also recently had to consider introducing a controversial green card scheme to attract IT specialists into the country.

The analysis is brought together in Chapter 6. Here it is argued that there are different trajectories of postindustrialism, and national models of capitalism exploit their competitive advantage by adapting in a variety of ways which are shaped by the institutional configurations. More significantly, it is emphasised that postindustrial transition is not uniform within Germany since there are a number of industrial and deindustrialised bases which are currently being subjected to change. In western Germany industrial production is being transformed. In the south-west of Germany this is being undertaken in a decentralised or networking fashion. In eastern Germany change is taking mostly the form of service sector employment or high-technology 'leapfrogging' postindustrial production, but not in a wholly successful way. A major problem is that Germany has resisted certain paths of postindustrial development, and regions which are not able to transform industrial production are constrained by the institutional framework which promotes this form of transformation. This chapter concludes the book with the argument that Germany will have to adapt its institutional framework so that its various postindustrial trajectories are accommodated and allowed to coexist on equal terms.

1
The German model . . . in crisis?

In the field of political economy capitalism has often been characterised in a way which involves mapping out the institutional differences between competing models of capitalism in order to explain their relative economic strengths and weaknesses (Shonfield 1965; Zysman 1983). The main distinction drawn is between liberal or market economies, state-led economies and co-ordinated or social market economies (Albert 1993; Coates 2000; Soskice 1999). The key differences between these forms of capitalism concern the respective relationships between the state and the market, between finance and industry, and between industry and labour. In short, in liberal economies these relationships are determined by the market, in state-led economies they are shaped by the state and in more co-ordinated economies they are characterised by negotiated, consensual settlements (Coates 1999; 2000). Further debates in the capitalist literature are concerned with 'periodising' capitalism (Coates 1999). This refers to discussions about what will happen to distinct models of capitalism as they pass into new phases of development. For example, Marxists divide the development of capitalism into three distinct phases – from feudal to capitalist to socialist economies – and the modernisation school identifies a progression from pre-industrial to industrial to post-industrial capitalist economy and society. While the tradition of classifying capitalist models emphasises the differences that exist between these capitalist arrangements, the periodiser approach tends to argue that these differences will be eradicated as capitalism converges towards a predetermined end state.

This book engages with both the traditions of modelling and of periodising capitalism. It is concerned both with the distinctiveness of the German model as well as with its fate in the emerging phase of postindustrial capitalism. It argues that this model of capitalism remains distinct and, despite the transition to a new phase of capitalism, there is little evidence of its convergence to other models of capitalism. This chapter begins with an account of the key features of the German model and assesses whether evidence from the 1990s confirms the view that this is in crisis. It then reviews some of the explanations for this crisis from two contrasting theoretical positions: the convergence perspective and an institutionalist perspective. Finally, while it broadly agrees with the institutionalist accounts, it highlights some of the limitations to these accounts.

The German model

It cannot be disputed that a distinct model of capitalism exists in Germany. Many of the features that make this model so distinctive date back to both the German industrial revolution and the Weimar Republic. However, as has been characterised in the models of capitalism literature, the German model generally refers to the set of arrangements that became institution-alised in the post-1945 period and led West Germany into a period of sustained economic growth, prosperity and stability. The German model tends, therefore, to refer to a specific period of West German industrialism. What are the classic features of the post-1945 German model?

German firms traditionally concentrate on the production and distribution of producer goods such as chemicals and heavy machinery. Many have an element of family management and most see themselves as social as well as economic institutions. As Streeck (1997: 241) puts it, they are 'social institutions, not just networks of private contracts or the property of their shareholders'. The social aspect of German firms is institution-alised by the ability of both capital and labour to participate in the everyday management of the firm. This requires decisions to be continuously negotiated and agreed by consensus. Capital is able to participate in the running of firms because German industry traditionally raises investment funds from universal banks in the form of long-term loans or credit (Zysman 1983). Banks in turn hold shares in the companies they support and are entitled to seats on their supervisory management boards. This enables banks to monitor the progress of the firms in which they have a stake and become better informed about the economic conditions in the industry and the degree of risk. This close interdependence encourages 'cradle to grave' relationships between firms and the institutions that fund them (Coates 2000: 67).

German labour is able to get involved in the running of firms by means of two institutions of codetermination (*Mitbestimmung*): it is represented on the company supervisory boards and through works councils on the shop floor (see Chapter 4). In addition, organised labour has the right to independent wage bargaining (*Tarifautonomie*). Trade unions negotiate collective agreements with employers' organisations and the agreement then becomes valid for the whole industry they represent. By setting wage levels through social partnership rather than allowing them to be determined by market forces, Germany has tended to be a high-wage economy in which firms are required to compete on quality and efficiency rather than on wages. High wages in industry are sustained by the fact that the German labour force is highly skilled and highly productive. The German education system has traditionally featured a strong 'dual' system of workplace and college-based training. Through this system, German firms invest in the training of the workforce and this encourages long-term employment relations (see Chapter 5).

The role of the state in the German model of capitalism can be characterised as 'neither *laissez-faire* nor *étatiste*' but rather as 'enabling' (Streeck 1997: 241). The state sets the framework that enables economic and social actors to govern themselves in organised and co-ordinated ways. The state is unable to direct the economy because of the fragmented nature of sovereignty in Germany. This is split horizontally (between federal government and independent authorities) and vertically (between federal government and the *Länder*). As Streeck (1997: 242) notes, this leads to 'both immobility and predictability of government policies, precluding rapid political innovation and allowing political agents to develop stable expectations, pursue long-term objectives and build lasting relations with one another'. There are a number of veto points in the German political system which makes socio-economic reform notoriously slow (Zohlnhöfer 2003).

These institutional features result in a model, which is sometimes labelled geographically as Rheinland or Rhenish capitalism (Albert 1993), but more often according to the distinct culture and set of principles which it breeds: the social market economy (Streeck 1997), a co-ordinated market economy (Soskice 1999), organised capitalism (Lash and Urry 1987), stakeholder capitalism (Hutton 1996) or trust-based capitalism (Coates 2000).

The crisis of models of capitalism

Since the start of the 1990s the institutional arrangements of the German model, once considered the driving force for Germany's strong economic performance in Europe and internationally, have come to be seen as the cause of Germany's comparatively poor economic performance. During the 1990s unemployment in Germany rose from 7.8 per cent in 1992 to 11.5 per cent in 1997 (Coates 2000: 5). This is partly explained by the recession of 1993 but, as Beck (1999: 1) notes, the scale of unemployment during this decade was more severe than during previous recessions. Moreover, some worrying structural trends developed. Long-term unemployment rose from 0.3 million in 1992 to 1.5 million in 1997 (Harding 1999: 70) and the distribution of unemployment in Germany was clearly regionally determined, with rates of unemployment in the east at twice the rate of those in the west and rates in the north significantly higher than in the south. There is also a gendered dimension to unemployment. Rates among men in 1999 were 9.4 per cent in the old *Länder* and 9.7 in the new *Länder*. The figures for women were 16.5 per cent and 21.6 per cent respectively (Beck 1999: 1–2). The higher unemployment rates among German women in the east reflect in part their higher labour market participation rates, but also the gendered outcomes of the economic transformation process that followed the collapse of the German Democratic Republic (GDR). The high rates of unemployment are explained by the loss of jobs in areas of traditional economic strength (Harding 1999: 70) and the failure to expand the labour market in the low-wage economy (see Chapter 3) and in new areas of economic activity such as information technologies (see Chapter 5).

The growth of the German economy stalled in the 1990s. Gross domestic product (GDP) growth per annum remained stable at 2.5 per cent but any expansion has tended to be driven by export performance rather than by domestic consumer demand (Harding 1999: 70). This figure also conceals an east–west difference (2.1 per cent and 2.7 per cent respectively). In May 2002 the European Commission estimated that two-thirds of the weak economic growth can be attributed to unification (cited in von Dohnanyi 2002). As a consequence of the high unemployment and low economic growth, government borrowing has been 'high and rising' since 1994 (Harding 1999: 70). Government spending has risen to meet the welfare spending commitments as well as its commitment to reconstructing the eastern part of Germany. Around 70 billion euros per year have been transferred to the east since 1990.

Many of the explanations for the poor performance of the German economy focused on the unsuitability of the German model to perform in the new period of capitalism. In 1990's Germany this crisis was referred to as the *Standortdebatte* or the debate about the efficiency of Germany as an industrial location given its existing institutional configuration. The debate was shaped by a vast literature which argued that models of capitalism that did not match the trend of the rapidly changing, market-led global economy would be obliged to transform in this direction in order to keep up. In most cases, the German model of capitalism was seen as one that would have to give way to more successful and appropriate institutional systems. Many have claimed that we are witnessing the demise of the consensual, co-ordinated German model and the victory of the more liberal free-market model of capitalism. They argue that the German model will not survive and is in demise because of technological developments, international competition and global capital markets.

The end of the German model? Convergence theories

Convergence theories predict that transformations of the capitalist system will eliminate the difference between national capitalist models and will lead to the emergence of a single economic and institutional model instead. This new model will either be the result of a narrowing of differences between two existing systems or a shift of all systems in a common direction (Kitschelt *et al.* 1999: 438). Early convergence theories such as those of the modernisation school argued that the logic of industrialism and the impact of universal technological forces would lead to convergence of capitalist and communist economies to a model of industrialism lying midway between the two economic systems (Galbraith 1967: 382–4; Kerr *et al.* 1973 cited in Waters 1995: 17).

Marxist and neoclassical economists ascribe universal laws to the development of socio-economic systems. They obviously have differing ideas of what the outcome will be but, as Hodgson (1999) argues convincingly, both these positions are teleological in nature as they assume a unitary end state towards which history is inevitably heading (see also Berger and Dore 1996). Neoclassical economists propose that market forces will ultimately lead capitalist economies to converge as a single liberal, free-market socio-economic arrangement. The logic of market competition will eradicate national capitalist models and will make regulated national economies the least competitive in a global economic system.

Marxist economists, on the other hand, argue that the contradictions inherent in the capitalist system will lead to the collapse of capitalism and convergence as a socialist economy. The collapse of real existing socialism in eastern Europe rendered two of these convergence theories obsolete. Convergence to a system midway between capitalism and communism was no longer possible since socialism was now neither real nor existing. Marxist theories of convergence were also discredited as the collapse of the socialist states of eastern Europe was evidence of their political and economical unsustainability. It was socialism, not capitalism, which collapsed under its inherent contradictions. That said, the collapse of actually existing socialism did not spell the absolute end to convergence theories. As Berger (1996: 4) notes, 'by the 1990s the idea that technology dictates a single optimal way of organizing production, thus propelling all countries toward common economic institutions and practices had largely vanished from the scene . . . The expectation that structures of production and the economy at large . . . are and should be converging is still alive and well today.' Indeed the collapse of the socialist alternative reinforced neoclassical theories of convergence and in the post-cold war era two convergence theories which predict convergence to free-market, neo-liberal conditions have been particularly strong: the end of history thesis and globalisation theory.

End of history convergence

An influential contribution to post-cold war convergence theory was provided by Fukuyama's much debated thesis that celebrated the demise of communism as the end of history. For Fukuyama (1992: 3), history, defined as 'a meaningful order to the broad sweep of human events' came to an end with the collapse of the USSR and the socialist states of eastern Europe. This development implies that 'the apparent number of choices that countries face in determining how they will organize themselves politically and economically has been *diminishing* over time' (45). All that is left is liberalism. In political terms this leaves states no alternative other than to organise along the lines of the 'decent and humane institutions of liberal democracy' (3). In economic terms the collapse of socialism meant states would necessarily become liberal economies (44). In the global context the events of 1989 marked the victory of liberal democracy over state socialism, capitalism over communism and free-market liberalism over more socially aware market forms. In Germany this development was seen in November 1989 when pressure from pro-democracy demonstrators led to the collapse of the socialist regime in the GDR. Less than a year later, on 3 October 1990, the GDR was officially dissolved and united with the liberal democratic and capitalist Federal Republic of Germany (FRG).

Globalisation

The 1990s marked the emergence of a new phase of capitalism which is characterised as a borderless world with international financial markets, global business competition and supranational economic governance institutions (Schmidt 1999). One school of globalisation theory – hyper-globalisation – unites orthodox neo-liberals and Marxists in the argument that globalisation defines a new economic era which is dominated by the global marketplace. Held *et al.* (1999: 3) argue that 'such a view of globalization generally privileges an economic logic and, in its neo-liberal variant, celebrates the emergence of a single global market and the principle of global competition as the harbingers of human progress'.

The most significant and forceful claim is that globalisation marks the end of national forms of governance and economic management. The outcome of the process of globalisation will be a 'borderless' economy in which 'national governments are relegated to little more than transition belts for global capital or, ultimately, simple intermediate institutions sandwiched between increasingly powerful local, regional and global mechanisms of governance' (Held *et al.* 1999: 3). The basic assumption is that in all industrialised states' firms are similar in terms of their basic structure and strategy. The competitiveness of these firms is, according to the globalisation thesis, clearly associated with their unit labour costs. It is assumed that firms in a global economy will move production abroad if labour costs are cheaper there. In order to persuade firms not to move, governments will be forced to alter their regulatory frameworks to make labour cheaper and more flexible and to reduce rates of taxation. In the global economy, resistance to measures such as these will come from labour and social democratic parties. However, because capital has more exit opportunities than labour, it is argued that labour is no longer able to shape national policies.

Neoclassical economists propose that globalisation is an evolutionary force which rewards efficient political economies and penalises inefficient ones (Kitschelt *et al.* 1999: 438). Therefore those which are not efficient in a free-market global environment will need to fall into line with the efficient ones. Market forces will ultimately lead capitalist economies to converge as a unitary, free-market socio-economic arrangement. The logic of market competition in the global economy will therefore eradicate national capitalist models and will make regulated national economies the least competitive in the global economic system. As Berger (1996: 2) puts it, 'the alternative capitalist systems that emerge . . . might satisfy national objectives, but at the expense of others in the international economic order'.

The implication of the convergence discourse in the globalisation literature for a co-ordinated or social market economy such as Germany's is clear. Streeck's (1997: 250–6) analysis of German capitalism in the 1990s holds the dynamics of globalisation responsible for its apparent crisis. While he acknowledges that there may have been a 'secular exhaustion' of the German model in the 1980s and that the institutional transfer associated with unification in 1990 placed additional pressure on the model, he ultimately argues that German capitalism is struggling because it has not met the demand imposed by globalisation that all capitalist systems conform to a single global norm. Since there is nothing about the German model which is efficient enough to be transferred to all models of capitalism globally, it will have to adapt itself to match the liberal model.

A defence of the German model: the importance of institutions

The theories of convergence, though ubiquitous and strong, do not stand up in the light of empirical evidence which shows the opposite result: that models of capitalism remained distinct in the globalised 1990s (Czada and Lütz 2000; Hall and Soskice 2001; Kitschelt et al. 1999). Alternative explanations emerged to explain why, despite the changing context, the models of capitalism appear to be resilient and do not converge to a single model but, rather, follow the paths on which they are developing and adapt where necessary. There are two main explanations for why differences persist: because of the embedded institutional frameworks which reinforce differences and because of the fact that political agency can still intervene to shape outcomes. The new institutionalist approach to political economy represents the counterposition to the teleological and deterministic claims made by convergence theorists. This section describes in detail institutionalist positions in political economy and then explains their perspectives on the end of history, globalisation and the crisis of the German model.

Institutions can be defined as the rules or constraints that we impose on ourselves. According to North (1990: 3) institutions are the 'humanly devised constraints that shape human interaction'. Institutions are created in order to reduce uncertainty and provide a structure to everyday life. According to North, institutions are important features of modern economies because they account not only for the different ways economies and societies are organised, but also for the different economic performances of economies. As North puts it, 'institutions affect the performance of the economy by their effect on the costs of exchange and production' (5). Institutions are developed to facilitate co-operation and cut down the costs of transaction.

North (1990) distinguishes between two kinds of institutions. *Formal* constraints are 'political (and judicial) rules, economic rules, and contracts' (47). *Informal* constraints, on the other hand, are 'codes of conduct, norms of behavior, and conventions' (36). These derive from information which is transmitted socially; they are 'part of the heritage that we call culture' (37). Together, informal and formal institutions shape the stability and economic performance of societies. As North notes, 'that the informal constraints are important in themselves (and not simply as appendages to formal rules) can be observed from the evidence that the same formal rules and/or constitutions imposed on different societies produce different outcomes' (36). Indeed, socio-economic outcomes are dependent on the interaction and interdependence of these two kinds of constraint. Formal and informal rules interact in a number of ways. For example, formal rules may be introduced to restrict the inefficiencies or corruption associated with informal institutions. They may 'be enacted to modify, revise, or replace informal constraints' (47). Alternatively, it may be the case that formal constraints provide a framework for informal activity as they 'lower information, monitoring, and enforcement costs and hence make informal constraints possible solutions to more complex exchange' (46–7). It is crucial to note the importance of informal institutions in their own right as factors which shape and define everyday interactions.

The central concept in theories of historical institutionalism is path dependence. This refers to the way in which decisions made at critical junctures in the past shape the characteristics and the scope of institutions in the present. Setterfield (1999: 841) offers the following definition:

> Economic outcomes are path dependent when they are fashioned, not just by activities and decisions in the present, but also by events that took place in the past. An economic outcome that is path dependent is the product of

the precise sequence of adjustments and changes that led up to it. Had this adjustment path been different, the specific outcome obtained would also be different.

New historical institutionalism is a reassertion of the view that history matters. This idea, as Setterfield (1999: 843) notes:

> has been elevated in recent developments in the principle of path dependence. Whether or not economists will now abandon thinking in terms of gravitation towards predetermined outcomes, in favor of thinking in terms of historical process and emergent properties, remains to be seen. What is certain is that historical and evolutionary processes are critical to political economy.

New institutionalists emphasise the role that institutions play in determining social and political outcomes (Hall and Taylor 1996: 936). It is argued that the contrasting institutional configurations which characterise states explain the existence and persistence of different social, political and economic outcomes. As Coates (1999: 647) notes, the new institutionalists are those economists, political scientists and sociologists who 'are committed to the notion of the necessary social embeddedness of all economic institutions, and to the resulting path-dependent and socially-specific nature of resulting economic trajectories'. Institutional frameworks of political economy provide a framework for specific kinds of activities: they shape economic growth and technological progress, and they determine the kind of innovation that takes place (Hall and Soskice 2001: 37–8). They provide comparative institutional advantage so that economies are able to develop to their own particular strengths. This facilitates the creation of niches of specialisation that distinct economies are able to pursue. Differing institutional configurations also mean that there will be different responses to similar sets of circumstances (Hall and Soskice 2001: 56).

Institutions and institutional frameworks provide for stability, and for this reason formal change is usually conducted incrementally; it is normally only visible as marginal adjustments along a given path. However, formal institutional change may also occur as a result of the activities of organisations, such as trade unions. These are created to take advantage of the opportunities which are determined by the existence of institutions in a society and 'as the organizations evolve, they alter institutions' (North 1990: 7). Where there has been incremental and negotiated change to formal institutions, it is usually the case that informal institutions adjust in parallel. A change in the formal constraints may initially result in a short-term situation of disequilibrium, but over the long term a renegotiation of the equilibrium between formal and informal institutions will evolve.

What happens, then, in instances of sudden or disruptive formal institutional change, for example, military conquest or revolution? In instances of rapid change to formal institutions, there will be a continuity of the informal, cultural institutional aspects of a society. Formal institutional change does not inscribe itself onto a 'clean slate', but rather against the background of historical legacies which shape informal institutions and cultural norms: in worlds which are 'already replete with institutions' (Hall and Taylor 1996: 953). Historical institutionalists are right to point to the tenacity of informal constraints, even when formal institutional change has been undergone. Informal constraints, which are culturally derived, will not alter in the short term in response to changes in the formal rules. In the short term there will be a tension between altered formal rules and persisting informal constraints (North 1990: 45). The informal rules retain an important function in the new formal institutional framework because 'they still resolve basic exchange problems among the participants, be they social, political, or economic' (91). Over time the process of renegotiation will lead to 'a restructuring of the overall constraints – in both directions – to produce a new equilibrium that is far less revolutionary' (91).

Institutionalism, the end of history and globalisation

From an institutionalist perspective, the collapse of the socialist states in 1989 does not entail the end of history. While it is true that these states abandoned their socialist economies and state forms and adopted liberal democracies and capitalist economies, there is no evidence that that this development was unitary and led to convergence in Europe – or globally – to a single political or economic model (Gamble 2000). Hodgson (1999) challenges the idea that the end of real existing socialism is the end of history or utopias. The collapse of socialism in eastern Europe has not automatically lead to free-market conditions. Hodgson claims that in its purest form free-market capitalism shares some inherent flaws with socialism, which makes it equally unsuitable for the contemporary economic era. Most significantly, both socialism and orthodox free-market approaches ignore the pluralism of institutional forms which shapes models of capitalism, and both are weak at innovating in the learning economy as they lack the diversity of approaches which drives innovation and learning. The evidence from the transition process in eastern Europe proves that there is nothing inevitable about processes of transition and that they are clearly still shaped by formal and informal institutions and political agency. Literature on the emerging capitalist economies in post-1989 eastern Europe 'confirms that path-dependent and historically contingent processes are leading, not to convergence to a presumed unique "Western" model, but to historically located and specific varieties of capitalism in each country' (Hodgson 1999: 151).

This can been seen most clearly in the transition of the political system and economy of the GDR. For very specific reasons, this collapse did not lead to the creation of a liberal economic system, but rather it adopted wholesale the social market model of the FRG. Rather than reconfiguring unified Germany as a new state, as provided for in Article 146 of the constitution, German unification was conducted according to Article 23 which allowed new *Länder* to join the FRG. This meant that following the collapse of the GDR the political and economic institutions were transferred wholesale in less than a year. The decision to unify in this way was clearly linked to Germany's common history and the dominant political will of East and West Germans in 1989 and 1990. The choice of integration process was a wholesale extension of the economic, legal, political and social institutions of West to East Germany. In the German context, the collapse of the socialist GDR marked the victory of the West German over the East German political and economic model. This is a clear-cut case of convergence to the West German model, not to liberal free-market capitalism, at precisely the time when the validity of such models was being called into question.

Institutionalists argue that political and economic features are shaped by both formal and informal rules which develop and change incrementally. Formal rules may change rapidly, but informal institutions are tenacious. What we see in unified Germany is wholesale transfer of the formal institutions of the German economic model, but not its perfect operationalisation. In eastern Germany formal institutions interact with, or are 'filled out' (Hyman 1996) by, the tenacious informal institutions in an attempt to make formal institutions work effectively (see Chapter 4). There have been many barriers to the full realisation of German–German convergence and many old 'national' differences remain. The case of German unification demonstrates that even when a single model of economic organisation is imposed on economic areas, formal and informal institutions protect difference and prevent convergence.

Institutionalist positions in the globalisation literature emphasise that economies will respond to the challenge of a globalised economy in various ways. The sceptical school argues that there is nothing new about globalisation and that contemporary levels of economic interdependence are not historically unprecedented and still national models emerge and are sustained (Hirst and Thompson 1996). They argue that globalisation is used as a rhetorical tool to implement otherwise unpopular economic reforms. The transformationalist school acknowledges that globalisation is a significant force that is reshaping modern societies and the world order, but do not accept that this will lead to global economic convergence or a single world society. Giddens (1994: 80) for example argues that globalisation is not just a force 'out there' but also an 'in here' phenomenon, meaning that global developments interact with local factors to shape the outcome. He argues 'we shouldn't think of globalization as a unitary process tending in a single direction, but as a complex set of changes with mixed and quite often contradictory outcomes' (80).

From an institutionalist perspective, the argument that models of capitalism that deviate from some global norm will hit a crisis is unsustainable. The economic advantage of states is bound up in the distinct institutional frameworks that have developed over the years and have given economies a niche in the global trading system and national economies will continue to adapt in path-dependent ways to the new challenges. Indeed, the evidence from the 1990s is that states have found different ways to do this and that their development is shaped by their respective configurations (Hall and Soskice 2001; Kitschelt *et al.* 1999; Scharpf and Schmidt 2000c). Scharpf and Schmidt (2000c) in fact go further. They argue that it is during periods of stability that national capitalisms appear to become more similar. What becomes apparent at times of change is how institutions at national level shape responses to the new challenges and the ways in which these responses differ.

Kitschelt *et al.* (1999: 441) find no evidence of convergence. They argue that 'for economic, organisational, and political reasons, it is unlikely that convergence will occur around any unique production regime and related configuration of social and political policies and institutions'. Coordinated economies remain as distinct as liberal market economies. Embedded forms of capitalism are less likely to diverge from the path upon which they are developing to converge with another model. In a state such as Germany the institutional framework of the economic model is particularly well embedded and there is little evidence that this is becoming dislodged (442). Institutions and economic linkages in systems of economic governance are tenacious (Coates 2000: 259) and there are often entrenched interests which prevent them from being undone. Soskice (1999) demonstrates the way in which Germany, which he characterises as a co-ordinated economy, is adapting in a co-ordinated manner. States can move from being vulnerable to competitive in the open economy without abandoning normative aspirations or jeopardising the legitimacy of governments (Scharpf and Schmidt 2000c: 20). However, it is also argued that while approaches to globalisation may differ and institutions may remain intact, states are nevertheless left with a narrower set of policy choices (Coates 2000; Scharpf and Schmidt 2000c). Coates also makes the point that while existing non-market models of capitalism will survive, there is no room for the development or emergence of new co-ordinated or trust-based capitalist models.

From the institutionalist perspective it can be argued that the crisis of the German model is not the consequence of its having failed to converge with a global norm. Nor is it about to disappear. In contrast to Streeck (1997), Harding (1999) sees no reason why it would not be possible for unified Germany to retain the national institutions of the German model in the global economy. She argues (Harding 1999: 81):

> there is no intrinsic reason why the German system should not be any less competitive that its American or British counterparts in the long term . . . Actors within the German economy are interrelated and interdependent through a system that has evolved and shown itself capable of incremental adaptation to exogenous radial change over centuries.

The crisis accounts, she argues, look at isolated indicators rather than assessing the system as a whole (67–8). By looking at the system as a whole, we are able to see a major, strong economy adapting successfully – if slowly – to change.

Limits to conventional defences of the German model

Institutional accounts which defend the German model are immensely valuable. They emphasise, rightly, that institutions embedded in the German model cannot be eradicated overnight. What is more, they suggest that the manner in which economic systems evolve in response to challenges such as globalisation are shaped by their institutional configurations. Yet, such accounts are not without their faults. Though worthy and important defences of the German model, they tend to defend and reinforce stylised accounts of the post-1945 West German political economy, which are limited in scope both geographically and conceptually. They fail to acknowledge the significant amount of diversity that exists historically within the German economy and as a consequence of unification. For example, Harding and Paterson (2000) offer an excellent and timely series of essays which provide overwhelming evidence in favour of the German model in the era of globalisation. They argue that while there are some worrying trends, there is real reason to be optimistic about the future of the German economy. However, their analysis focuses on how well the institutions of the German model function in the traditional industrial areas of the Germany economy and it does not attempt to account for the variations within Germany. Crucially, Harding and Paterson exclude the new *Länder* from their analysis on the grounds that the book deals mainly with the impact of one exogenous shock on the German model (globalisation). Alternatively, accounts which highlight the success of regional districts such as Baden-Württemberg either deal with this phenomenon in isolation without stating the implications for the German model as a whole or assume that the successful strategy of flexible specialisation can be generalised to the whole of the political economy.

The following discussion addresses the gap left by many conventional defences of the German model. This book seeks to account for the variation within the model and the impact that this has on the performance of the German economy. The argument put forward here is that the German economy and the German model have been affected by the changing context associated with globalisation and post-communist transition in a way which has led to increased diversity within the national political economy. The next section, therefore, maps out the plurality of capitalist paths or trajectories which exist in unified Germany today. These trajectories derive from different paths to industrialisation, the experience of German division and unification, and the developments since 1990. The picture that emerges depicts a plurality of regional capitalist trajectories which coexist within unified Germany.

Regional diversity of German capitalism

Gary Herrigel's (1996) seminal study on the sources of German industrial power provides an excellent starting point from which to identify different capitalist trajectories in unified Germany. Herrigel rejects conventional accounts of the political economy of industrial Germany (Gerschenkron

1962; Schumpeter 1947), which came to dominate debates in the post-1945 period on the grounds that they tend to depict a highly centralised, large-firm dominated, neo-corporatist industrial system. These conventional 'organised capitalism' accounts are, Herrigel argues, deeply flawed positions since they refer to, and stylise, just one of two industrial orders which coexist in Germany. To counter such unitary characterisations of German industrialism, Herrigel traces the development, from industrialisation to the mid-1990s, of two distinct German orders of industrialism: the decentralised and the autarkic. His detailed analysis illustrates how these two distinct historical origins of German industrialism have continued to shape industrialism, despite efforts at different historical junctures to create a unitary or centralised industrial regime. Herrigel argues that conventional, unitary accounts of German industrialism focus solely on the autarkic order during the post-1945 period and that the decentralised industrial tradition is 'blended out' or misrepresented.

The first and oldest regional system on the German territory identified by Herrigel is the *decentralised* industrial order. This is 'composed of multitudes of highly specialised small- and medium-sized producers and a host of extra firm-supporting institutions' which operate as a system of production across a whole region rather than within the boundaries of a firm. The actors in this system are mutually interdependent and they have together 'created a system of governance mechanisms that stimulate innovation, socialise risk, and foster adjustment' (Herrigel 1996: 1–2). The industrialisation of decentralised regions began early; shortly after the Thirty Years War (1618–48), and well before the industrial revolution. Through the process of industrialisation, regional economies emerged, each with unique and specialised products which helped individual regions adapt to changes in the world markets and to create niche markets. The origins of the decentralised industrial order can be found in regions that had property relations favouring peasants (34). The latter were able to assert strong claims to the land on account of inheritance rights which divided land between all children in a family. Peasants in these regions benefited from these rules in two ways. They were able to engage in minor industrial employment on their land as well as in farming. Also they were never 'propertyless' and so were not placed in the vulnerable position of having to become factory labourers (35). Herrigel identifies the following regions as decentralised: 'the western and southern portions of what ultimately became the old Prussian Rheinprovinz, portions of western and southern Hesse, Baden and Württemberg in the southwest, the lower part of the Main and the upper

Franconian regions of northern Bavaria, the Kingdom of Saxony, and the Thüringen States' (34).

The second regional system described by Herrigel is the *autarkic* industrial order which is characterised by very large-scale, vertically integrated enterprises. By autarky Herrigel (1996) means the fact that 'nearly all tasks directly involved with production and its governance [are organized] within the boundaries of the firm'. By using the term 'autarky' Herrigel does not mean to imply that such firms had no external ties whatsoever, but intends to stress the fact that the factory site is relied upon for all aspects of production and related production tasks, such as marketing and sales, rather than spreading these out over a number of interrelated producers in a regional system (75). The autarkic industrial order emerged at the time of the second industrial revolution (1830–70) in regions where there had previously been no industrial activity. Autarkic firms were able to emerge in such areas and they had two advantages. Firstly, property relations had prevented peasants owning property and this meant there was no shortage of factory recruits. Secondly, they were able to develop rapidly by capitalising on the innovations of states, such as Britain and Belgium, which had already been industrialised. The ability of these autarkic firms to start from scratch was to their distinct advantage, in fact, the advantage German industrialism had from this 'late' route to industrialisation has been cited frequently as the reason for its ongoing strength as an industrial economy. Gerschenkron (1962), for example, argues that German capitalism was characterised by 'backwardness' until the development of large autarkic firms. He argued that the Germans turned their own backwardness to their advantage by constructing, unhindered by the competition of small firms, large, superbly efficient plants which produced to the highest international standards.

Most conventional accounts of German industrialism are dominated by the autarkic industrial order. Herrigel's 1996 study, by contrast, illustrates how the two industrial orders have in fact successfully coexisted over time within the institutional framework of the nation state. Furthermore, he attributes the success of the German political economy to this very coexistence of different systems of regionally differentiated industrial practice (autarkic and decentralised). The autarkic and decentralised industrial orders have been successfully governed within a single national political economy through *accommodation* and *coexistence*. Accommodation refers to 'the successful provision by a particular historical regime of the mechanisms necessary for the stable reproduction of an industrial order'. Coexistence refers to 'the stable reproduction of both forms of industrial order within the political and economic boundaries defined by a given historical German regime' (112). In Germany, a governance system which allows for a high degree of self-government at regional level, has accommodated industrial orders so that they may coexist. This has been achieved through a heterogeneity of governance that exists at regional and industrial levels in Germany which also exists at the national level in the form of a 'nonintegrated, composite architecture of national industrial governance structures' (2).

Herrigel argues that the success of accommodation and coexistence has varied over time and has been dependent on different political regimes. At different junctures of history, for example when political or economic regimes have changed, accommodation and coexistence between these orders have been renegotiated. Over time the relationship of the respective orders towards each other, as well as towards the state, has changed. This can be generally characterised by the decentralised regions defending their regional autonomy and the autarkic regions resisting regulatory interference from the central state, while at the same time making use of the improved national infrastructures.

Herrigel's approach is an invaluable starting point for characterising the complexity of German capitalism today. Yet it is not a wholly adequate framework as his coverage of the post-1945 period focuses solely on West Germany and this present study is interested in identifying the complexity of capitalism in unified Germany. It is necessary, therefore, to build on Herrigel's work by blending in the industrial experience of the GDR and the industrial characteristics of the new *Länder* since 1989/90. To characterise and understand the features of the new *Länder* Herrigel's industrial constructions approach is supplemented by the key historical events of the socialist industrial experience and the economic transformation which followed the *Wende* and unification.

Herrigel excludes the eastern part of Germany from his analysis of the post-1945 period. Yet his pre-1933 analysis reveals that eastern Germany (that is, the area that became the GDR) was traditionally divided equally into three regions: the agrarian region in the north, the autarkic region in the centre and the decentralised region in the south. Between 1945 and 1989, this traditional configuration of eastern Germany changed in a number of ways on account of the impact of state socialism, the industrial decline following the *Wende* and the outcome of the slow economic recovery of the 1990s. During the forty-year history of the GDR three developments can be identified. Firstly, in the early phases of socialist industrialisation in the GDR a large area of previously agrarian and non-industrialised eastern

Germany was industrialised. Secondly, much of the autarkic industrial base which had existed up until 1945–49 was destroyed during the war and the socialist regime of the GDR re-established this industrial base according to centralised, socialist principles. East German firms were reorganised in a large-scale, autarkic manner. In 1987 a larger percentage of East Germans were employed in industry and in agriculture than in the west. In 1988, 75.7 per cent of GDR mining and manufacturing workers were in enterprises employing over 1000 employees. The figure in the west was 39.3 per cent. (Lange and Shackleton 1998: 90).

The third trend in the GDR was a gradual dismantling of the decentralised industrial region. The socialist industrial ideology and industrial policies of the GDR favoured state-owned, large-scale enterprises. Small and medium-sized enterprises (SMEs) were nationalised and integrated into the state-owned enterprises. The decentralised tradition lost its economic and cultural significance and was rendered almost wholly extinct. The nationalisation of the East German decentralised regions was undertaken gradually. Prior to the construction of the Berlin Wall in 1961 their survival was, to a certain degree, protected by an industrial and political concern to stem the exodus of the high-skilled *Mittelstand* from the GDR. During the 1960s, most SMEs were transformed into 'half state-owned' enterprises: they survived, but not autonomously. By 1972 nearly all of the remaining 'half state-owned' enterprises had been completely nationalised. Despite the centralising industrial policies, however, a small number of privately owned SMEs survived until 1989. One way to account for this is that they existed 'to reduce supply bottlenecks for the population in particular fields' (Nicolai 1998: 75). However the significance of residual SMEs should not be overstated: by 1989 only 11 per thousand of the population were self-employed and seven per thousand were craftspeople (Merk 1994, cited in Nicolai 1998: 76).

The gradual, ideologically driven removal of the more flexible decentralised industrial order in East Germany made it harder for the east to adapt to the economic challenges of the 1970s and 1980s. An increasingly global product market and the introduction of new technologies required firms to adapt rapidly and flexibly, but the rigid, autarkic structures of the GDR firms prevented it from doing this. As outlined above, the autarkic firms in the west were able to adapt to the new phase of capitalism by subcontracting out to smaller supporting firms. The failure of the GDR to respond reflexively and to adapt in an innovative way to the changing nature of global industrialism certainly contributed to its demise. The collapse of the autarkic industrial order meant that the

GDR was no longer able to sustain its political aims. The GDR collapsed and following unification the GDR economy, dominated by large, state-owned, centrally run *Kombinate* was transformed into a capitalist market system. One of the major tasks of unification was to break up and privatise the autarkic, state-run enterprises. This task was approached through the agency *Treuhand* (trustee office) 'by a combination of methods: returning some establishments to former owners, finding private buyers for others, transferring some to local authorities, and closing others down altogether' (Hyman 1996: 3). By the time *Treuhand* wound up its business in the mid-1990s there had been a large-scale destruction of the former East German economic base. Industrial production had declined by 70 per cent and there had been an almost total deindustrialisation of some parts of eastern Germany (Hyman 1996: 4) (see Chapter 4).

From this historical review of the different paths or trajectories of German industrialism it becomes apparent that contemporary capitalism in unified Germany is more complex than most conventional, and indeed even more differentiated, accounts such as Herrigel's suggest. The first aim of this book is to challenge these existing accounts and to highlight the different economic trajectories that coexist within unified Germany today.

Postindustrial transition and German capitalism

The second aim of this book is to challenge the traditional accounts of the German model, which specifically focus on it as an industrial economy. A number of institutional defences of the German model tend to emphasise continuity and stability in order to make the point that the model is still relevant and significant. In so doing the assumption is made that German capitalism and the German model today are a continuation of what came before. A balance needs to be struck between the accounts which insist on stating difference and the view that capitalist systems develop through distinct periods of development. What is missing is a dynamic account which emphasises the durability of competing capitalist institutional frameworks, but acknowledges that national political economies are systems that experience external shocks and undergo processes of transformation which upset the equilibria of those systems and demand adjustment, which in turn will be oriented to the institutional re-creation of comparative advantage. Old forms of divergence persist and new forms of divergence emerge as political economies respond to new challenges.

There are no stable sets of policies and institutions in any country that are well adapted to the new era. Instead there is change in all countries and regions, and these are adapting in different ways (Kitschelt *et al.* 1999: 457). Some accounts do stress the fact that as economic systems enter new phases of development they do not converge but do remain distinct, and may even become more diverse (Scharpf and Schmidt 2000c). This book looks at the impact of postindustrial transformation of models of capitalism, and on the regional postindustrial trajectories within unified Germany. To do this it is first necessary to elaborate on what is meant by postindustrialism.

2

Defining postindustrialism: service sector, technological transformation and knowledge

Models of capitalism do not remain stuck in a fixed point of historical development. As Hodgson (1999: 181) argues, 'modern, developed economies have entered, in the last two decades of the twentieth century, a long process which can lead to immense transformations, of historical proportions compared to the Industrial Revolution itself'. Manuel Castells (1996: 29) similarly claims that 'at the end of the twentieth century, we are living through one of these rare intervals in history' which is marked by 'major events that occur with great rapidity and help to establish the next stable era'. Postindustrialism is an extensive body of theory which is concerned with explaining, and sometimes forecasting, the transition of advanced industrial economies to a new phase of economic development. It deals with the impact of this transition on the economy, society, institutions of work and identities.

The concept of the postindustrial economy and society has taken a number of different forms and these are critically reviewed in this chapter. The chapter contrasts three of the ways in which the postindustrial political economy has been conceptualised: as a shift from a manufacturing to a service sector economy (Bell 1974; Esping-Andersen 1990); as a transformation of systems of industrial production from mass production to flexible specialisation as a consequence of technological developments (Amin 1994; Castells 1996; Sabel 1994, 1995; Soskice 1999); and as the knowledge economy (Berger 1996; Hodgson 1999).

The literature on postindustrial transition is divided between those who assert that the postindustrial transformation will result in a convergence of models of capitalism to a single model and those who believe that institutions embedded at the national level will shape the outcomes of the postindustrial state. Since the 1970s theories about postindustrial economy were dominated by the view that the next phase of economic development would bring economies together to some predetermined end point. Each theory emphasised a different vision of the postindustrial economy and society (Kumar 1996). One set of theories emphasised a singular shift from manufacturing to a service sector economy (Bell 1996). In a postindustrial society, there would be activity in the service sector rather than in manufacturing. New jobs are created in either the low-wage service economy or in the higher-wage knowledge economy. Alternatively, there are theories which emphasise the way in which the economy and its industrial production is responding and transforming in the light of technological innovations. For example, post-Fordism highlighted the new production methods (flexible specialisation) which were being developed in certain areas such as Northern Italy and Baden-Württemberg (Amin 1994; Hall 1988; Murray 1988; 1991). Chapter 2 proposes an inclusive and complex version of postindustrial transition that, firstly, involves both an increase in but not a complete transformation to service sector activity, the transformation of national production systems and the increased significance of knowledge. It is also argued that there is no single model of the postindustrial economy. Rather it is clearly shaped by the formal and informal institutions which exist at national and regional levels and will develop in a path-dependent way.

The service sector economy

An economy dominated by the service sector has been the most common approach to postindustrial theory. It predicts an evolutionary process of development from employment in agriculture to manufacturing and, in a final stage, to services. Fourastié (1969) predicted that because of technological innovations in the primary and secondary sectors, by the end of the twentieth century, 80 per cent of employment would be in the service sector. Similar predictions were made by Bell (1974), although he specifically argued that employment would become concentrated in the high-skilled, high-knowledge and high-wage service sector activity. The service sector economy then became the dominant version of the postindustrial future. A state able to rapidly expand service employment should be considered an advanced postindustrial economy.

While service sector employment has certainly increased rapidly, it has not quite been in line with the predictions made by Fourastié or Bell. Dathe and Schmid (2000: 4) succinctly summarise the key three arguments which temper any kind of optimism about the service sector postindustrial economy. Firstly, innovations such as personal computers and washing machines mean that many traditional services have been transformed into manufactured goods used for self-servicing. Secondly, since individual time budgets are limited, the consumption of services are also limited. Thirdly, since services are not as productive as manufacturing, wages in services will tend to be set at a lower rate than in productive occupations. This can lead to large wage differentials in postindustrial economies, which some economies may be keen to resist.

What is more, service sector employment has developed in different ways and at different speeds in advanced capitalist states. Esping-Anderson (1990) differentiated between three models of service sector postindustrial development. In the liberal model, provision of services is regulated by markets and services develop in two opposing ways. On the one hand, a knowledge service economy develops which is marked by highly qualified and highly paid jobs mostly in the high-technology communication areas of economic activity. On the other hand, a low-skill, low-wage service economy develops. Since in service industries labour costs represent a high proportion of total cost, in an unregulated market, wages are kept to a minimum so as to maximise profits. Furthermore, the nature of jobs created in the service sector here is more flexible than in the industrial sector and a high proportion of the work is part time and undertaken by women. This too helps to keep the labour costs to a minimum. The result is the development of a strongly polarised postindustrial society as has been seen in the USA and the UK.

The social democratic trajectory represents the opposite end of the postindustrial spectrum. This model is characterised by a rapid expansion of the service sector in the 1980s but in the form of public services such as education, health and childcare which were funded by public resources. In states like Sweden the service sector came to provide secure and protected employment for a highly qualified and largely female workforce. As in the liberal model there are large wage differentials between the male-dominated private sector and the female-dominated public sector, but these are not as wide.

The corporatist model of postindustrial development is characterised by a reduction of industrial employment but a slow expansion of service employment. Germany, as an example of a corporatist state, is characterised as being 'peculiar in that its "post-industrial" employment-growth is sluggish, be it in producer, social, or "fun" services' (Esping-Anderson 1990: 198). This trend is accounted for in a number of ways. Firstly, in corporatist welfare states, such as Germany, services are, in accordance with the principle of subsidiarity, traditionally provided informally or within the family. Hence the state has been reluctant to provide the kinds of service which encourage women to take up employment (224). Secondly, wage policies and high fixed labour costs in corporatist states prohibit a growth of low-wage service sector employment. The response to the decline in industrial employment has been to limit access to the labour market through early retirement and long periods of education. Esping Andersen proposes 'the main prognosis for the German trajectory, then, is that Germany will remain predominantly an industrial economy, but with diminishing numbers of people involved in production, and an ever-increasing population of housewives, the young, and the elderly excluded from employment and dependent on the welfare state'. It will be a 'work-less world'. (214). He warns that this could lead to an 'insider–outsider' scenario whereby 'collective negotiations are conducted solely on behalf of those with jobs, pursuing wage maximisation at the expense of job expansion for the outsiders' (227). This could in turn lead to a crisis of welfare legitimacy as the core workers might be less inclined to support those not active in the labour market.

Iverson and Wren (1998) argue that the development towards a service economy presents states with a trilemma. In the industrial era states were able to pursue simultaneously the goals of budgetary restraint, income equality and employment growth. In the service economy it is only possible to pursue two of these and states have made different choices regarding the direction they take: liberal service economies have prioritised budgetary restraint and employment growth at the expense of income equality; social democratic service economies have opted for income equality and employment growth at the expense of budgetary restraint; and the corporatist service economy has favoured budgetary restraint and income equality at the expense of employment growth.

Concerns about the limited capacity of conservative states to create new employment has led to end-of-work theories which argue that the postindustrial society is characterised by the end of industrial and industrialised work. This vision of the postindustrial state originated in the late nineteenth century from the utopian socialist William Morris who foresaw 'an economy of small-scale, workshop-based craft production' in which workers would have control over their means of production (Edgar and Sedgewick 1999: 293). Contemporary end-of-work theorists fall into two categories. On the one hand, there are the postindustrial utopians. This is a group of theorists (Gorz, Bahro and Toffler) who have a vision of postindustrial society as an ecologically sound, socialist utopia (Frankel 1987:

245). The shift to postindustrial conditions is triggered by both the inability of industrial regimes to maintain the required levels of economic growth and on account of the ecological damage caused by industrialism. The postindustrial socialist society is not centrally organised as industrial socialist states were. Rather, the alternative proposition is a decentralised postindustrial society inhabited by autonomous citizens in small communities. Postindustrialism is regarded by utopian thinkers as the opportunity to renew enlightenment hopes of self-fulfilment with the prosperity of the industrial age. Some argue that postindustrialism re-establishes that link between work and identity, that is to say, people are no longer alienated by their work. Moreover, in such a society, labour would have more autonomy over their economic activity, and this renders the working class extinct as everyone is in charge of their own labour.

The second, more dystopian, end-of-work thesis has been proposed by Jeremy Rifkin (1996; 1997) and Ulrich Beck (1998). These positions both assert that postindustrial technological revolutions have rendered human work unnecessary, and that the only future of work lies in the third sector, voluntary activities. Jeremy Rifkin's end-of-work thesis claims that technological innovations and developments render labour, as a factor of production, extinct. Rifkin believes that 'now, for the first time, human labor is being systematically eliminated from the production process' (Rifkin 1996: 3). His argument (xv) is that:

> new, more sophisticated software technologies are going to bring civilization ever closer to a near workerless world . . . The wholesale substitution of machines for workers is going to force every nation to rethink the role of human beings in the social process . . . Redefining opportunities and responsibilities for millions of people in a society absent of mass formal employment is likely to be the single most pressing issue of the coming century.

The end of work will, Rifkin claims, pose severe difficulties for industrial states which have been structured on work and workers whose worth has been measured by the market value of their labour (xviii). Of particular concern is the potential of high levels of unemployment to create social and political unrest that might endanger democracy.

While it seems that some states have indeed experienced problems creating new employment in services, this does not necessarily imply the end of work. Nor does it mean that such states have exhausted all possibilities of expanding employment in services. Esping-Andersen (1999; 2002) has recently argued that service sector employment could, and should, be expanded by encouraging women to enter the labour market. Increasing levels of female employment is thought to have significant potential to increase overall levels of service sector employment. If women in male breadwinner states are expected to work, then demand will be created for additional formal professional jobs to carry out the work that women used to do otherwise informally (e.g. childcare, care for the elderly). In addition, it is anticipated that this transition could create additional low-wage jobs in the areas of private household services as women will have less time to work in the public and private spheres. This raises a number of issues among feminists. There is a paradox that women will not be paid to look after their own families, but they would be paid to look after those of others. Also, there is a concern that much of the low-wage employment that emerges will be taken up by women and that economic equalities and dependencies will still exist.

Technological transformation

An alternative way of conceiving of the postindustrial economy is by looking at the impact of technological transformations on industrial production. It might be the case that service employment remains low because there is a transformation rather than an elimination of industrial production, or that services are linked to industrial production rather than existing independently in the service sector. One of the first approaches to consider this phenomenon was post-Fordism (Amin 1994; Kumar 1996). This school of thought analysed the shift away from Fordism, whereby firms were able to deliver standardised goods cheaply through mass production, to a post-Fordist regime in which goods were being produced according to the principle of flexible specialisation. This meant that new technologies could be used to change production techniques in order to match rapidly changing consumer demands. The principle of flexible specialisation also requires highly skilled workers who are able to adapt to, and even initiate, new production techniques to meet shifting consumer demands. However, the post-Fordist paradigm only ever related to specific regions such as the 'Third Italy' which were identified as areas particularly suited to adapting to changing consumer demand. The 'Third Italy' term was coined to distinguish the area from the 'First Italy' of large-scale mass production concentrated in the industrial triangle of Turin, Milan and Genoa and the 'Second Italy' of the mezzogiorno – the economically underdeveloped South (Kumar 1996: 37–8). Others authors identified areas such as the south-west of Germany as being particularly strong in the shift to flexible specialisation (Sabel 1989; 1995). While those from the post-Fordist school anticipated that the paradigm of flexible specialisation could be generalised to all advanced economies, others realised that there was something specific about these regions which enabled them to transform in this way (Sabel 1994). Other regions would not necessarily be able to emulate this.

Castells (1996), too, looks at the way economies are being transformed through the period of rapid restructuring triggered by the Information Technology Revolution (ITR) since the 1970s. Castells rejects the idea that this new era is marked by a shift from manufacturing to services. While he recognises that in advanced economies there has been a notable decline in manufacturing and a growth in service sector activities, he argues that 'it does not follow that manufacturing industries are disappearing or that the structure and dynamics of manufacturing activity are indifferent to the health of the service economy' (205). Castells also rejects postindustrial accounts which claim that productivity and growth are promoted by the generation of knowledge. He rejects the proposition that the new economy would increase the importance of occupations with a high information and knowledge content in their activity such as managerial, professional and technical occupations (103–4). Castells stresses that the growth of the low-end, unskilled, service sector occupations could become increasingly significant and provide for a more polarised social structure, 'where the top and the bottom increase their share at the expense of the middle' (206).

In contrast to the post-Fordist school, Castells does not assume that all economies will transform in the same way, or that there will be a complete break from one historical period to the next. Rather, the impact of the ITR is to transform aspects of an economy, society and culture in path dependent ways. The ITR is not then a shift to another historical period, rather it is a transformation of the current era in the light of new technological developments. This is no minor transformation however. Castells asserts that the transforming impact of the ITR is in fact more disruptive and pervasive to our social and economic systems and more significant to our society than were the first and second industrial revolutions (30). While the developments of the Industrial Revolution took hundreds of years to develop and disseminate (32–3), the impact of the ITR has been concentrated into a much shorter period: the last thirty years of the twentieth century. Also, the ITR is more disruptive and pervasive than the Industrial Revolution because of its ability to overcome the constraints of physical space, thereby ensuring the immediate spread of IT to almost all corners of the globe (33–4).

This approach to postindustrialism implies that all states are affected but that their transformation takes different forms. Castells suggests the way in which employment and occupational structures are organised, as well as the sectors in which most service sector employment is carried out, will differ from state to state. Thus, the outcome of the transition of advanced industrial societies through the ITR is three distinct models of informational.

The Service Economy Model is characterized by Castells (1996) as 'an entirely new employment structure where the differentiation among various service activities becomes the key element to analyze social structure' (229). In this model, manufacturing employment decreased rapidly after 1970 as the pace towards informationalism accelerated and, as a consequence, the kind of services that become significant are capital management services rather than producer services. In addition, the social service sector becomes increasingly important because of a sharp rise in healthcare jobs and, to a lesser extent, in education employment. It is also characterized by the 'expansion of the managerial category that includes a considerable number of middle managers' (229). Typical examples of the Service Economy Model are the USA, the UK and Canada (229).

The second model that Castells identifies is the Industrial Production Model. In this model, manufacturing activities have been restructured to adapt to the new sociotechnical paradigm rather than rapidly scaled down. Indeed, the share of manufacturing employment remains at a high level: around one-quarter of the labour force (229–30). This model in fact reduces manufacturing jobs while reinforcing manufacturing activity. The kind of service activity that emerges is in the form of producer services that directly support manufacturing activity rather than financial services. Castells is careful to point out that 'this is not to say that financial services are not important . . . Yet, while financial services are indeed important and have increased their share in both countries, the bulk of service growth is in services to companies' (230). Two states which fit clearly into this model are, according to Castells, Japan and Germany (229).

Castells adds, somewhat more tentatively, a third model. This is a model of informationalism in which almost one-quarter of employment is on a self-employed basis and by 'different organizational arrangements, based on networks of small and medium businesses' (230). What is distinctive about this model is the way in which these networks of SMEs have successfully adapted, through the ability to innovate rapidly to changing consumer tastes and the rapidly changing conditions of the global economy thus 'laying the ground for an interesting transition from proto-industrialism to proto-informationalism' (230). Castells does not give this model a name, but it will be referred to here as the Networking Model. Castells identifies Italy as the state which represents this model.

Castells is certainly right to point out how national models of capitalism adapt to the ITR in distinct, path-dependent ways. The different institutional configurations of models of capitalism clearly set paths of transformation so that there is a complex or diverse pattern of postindustrial transition. However, there appears to be an additional level of complexity to this kind of postindustrial transition that Castells does not deal with: there are clearly distinct regional postindustrial developments within nation states. This regional dimension can be best illustrated by looking more closely at the Networking Model that Castells identifies in Italy. What he identifies is a model that certainly does not apply to the whole of the very diverse Italian economy but, rather, to the prosperous regions in the centre and north-east regions of Italy (Tuscany, Umbria, the Marche, Emilia-Romagna, Veneto, Friuli, Trentino-Alto Adige), also known as the 'Third Italy'. Within Italy, then there are clearly distinct postindustrial trajectories which coexist.

In addition to Castells's analysis there are states which experience technological transformations and the collapse of the industrial mass production paradigm at the same as the collapse of political and economic institutions. For example, Norton-Standen (1997) proposes that, as a consequence of the upheavals of 1989 and the transition period of the 1990s, the ex-socialist states of eastern Europe have lost both their industrial base and the industrial institutions which had developed with it. The lack of industrial 'baggage' – industrial institutions and entrenched industrial mindsets – allows these states to 'leapfrog' into the postindustrial age. Leap-frogging theory proposes that if states experience postindustrial transformation at the same time as political and economic revolution then they will be better placed to adapt to a new socio-economic paradigm.

Norten-Standen demonstrates that the postindustrial transformation of the ex-socialist states of eastern Europe is proceeding at a fast rate. The eastern European states are seeking to 'compress 30 years of business evolution in the West into five to seven years of business revolution in eastern Europe'. These economies are replacing and renewing their infrastructures with business practices from the Information Technology Revolution.

Major industries . . . most particularly the banking, finance, telecommunications and media sectors, are already using the very latest technology to
drive it forward competitively. In doing so, these organisations have not
been hampered by existing technology infrastructures and have been able to
immediately implement technology that is more up to date than some
western businesses.

Moreover, there is less resistance to the implementation of new methods
and technologies. Norton-Standen notes that there is a business revolution in these transforming economies which is characterised by a 'fundamental change in business practice and a lack of entrenched business or
social mind-set'.

Thus, Norten-Standen proposes that eastern European states have a
comparative advantage. Western European states 'such as Britain, France
and Germany have been able to pursue comprehensive social revolutions
based on financial muscle' but at the same time they have retained, and
are restrained by, the formal and informal institutions of the industrial
era. In contrast, eastern European states have had to 'pursue comprehensive social change based on social muscle': they have experienced postindustrial transformation at the same time as they have renewed their
formal and informal institutions. Without this baggage, they can leapfrog
into the postindustrial age.

Yet from a more institutional perspective, the leapfrogging theory does
not stand up. Transformed states are not able to start with a clean slate but
rather, as Hodgson (1999: 147) argues, 'each system is obliged . . . to build
out of the remaining bric-à-brac of the past. All development is a process
of creatively "making do" with the historical legacy of institutions and
routines. We can never build anew'.

The knowledge economy

Knowledge has always been central to innovation and economic development. Knowledge-based economies are ones in which investment in the
production and reproduction of knowledge has become the key to promoting economic growth. As Steinmueller (2002: 142) points out,
'knowledge contributes to the economy by supporting productivity
improvements, the formation and growth of new industries, and the
organisational changes that are needed to effectively utilise the new
knowledge.' Similarly, knowledge economies are ones in which large numbers of workers deal with information rather than tangibles. Theories

of the knowledge economy recognise that the production and reproduction of knowledge lie at the heart of economic growth and that the ability to invest and innovate is what fuels development. Knowledge has, arguably, always been important in the development of economies. What is new in the current era of economic development is the accelerated speed at which knowledge is created, accumulated and depreciates (David and Foray 2002).

The productivity and growth of economies has less to do with investment in resources and more to do with the capacity of that state to improve human capital. What is crucial is a state's capacity to create new knowledge and ideas and to incorporate them into equipment and people. Investment is therefore less crucial in tangible capital (infrastructure and equipment) and more crucial in intangible capital, meaning human capital. This can take the form either of producing and sustaining human capital through education and training or sustaining it through investment in health and welfare (David and Foray 2002).

What appears to be crucial for the knowledge economy is the kind of human capital that is created. What is emphasised in theories of the knowledge economy is the kind of human capital skills that are required to facilitate the rapid production and reproduction of knowledge. David and Foray (2002) argue that technical skills are less important than generic learning skills. What is crucial is the capacity to understand and anticipate change. It is also crucial to promote teamwork and communication skills in order to aid the development of new institutions to facilitate the production and reproduction of knowledge. What is required is knowledge-based communities which bring together networks of individuals from business, science and politics, cutting across boundaries of conventional organisations to create a public space for the exchange and dissemination of knowledge.

It is important to distinguish between information and knowledge. Information refers to data to which some meaning has been attributed, whereas knowledge can be defined as the product of information use (Hodgson 1999: 46). Alternatively, information can be taken as meaning knowledge that has been codified. In order to pass on knowledge, it needs to be codified, or transformed into manageable and communicable pieces of information. Knowledge that cannot be codified and transferred is referred to as tacit knowledge. Tacit knowledge includes, for example, skills that are acquired through practice and can only be passed on in situations of social interaction such as during an apprenticeship. In the knowledge economy, it become important to acquire new knowledge and skills through continual processes of learning. Hodgson (1999: 247–8) defines learning as more than the mere acquisition of knowledge. He characterises learning as a process of problem-defining and problem-solving. Moreover, he differentiates between simple learning and second-order learning, the latter being the ability to learn how to learn. This has filtered through to policy-making circles as the concept of 'lifelong learning'.

Daniel Bell's (1974) futuristic predictions or forecasts about the coming of a postindustrial society were constructed on one such vision of a knowledge economy. Bell distinguishes between three historical periods – the pre-industrial society, the industrial society and the postindustrial society (116). Each of these is constructed around the concept of an 'axial principle' which is a conceptual schema or an organising frame (10). Pre-industrial societies are concerned with the production of food and other natural products required for self-sustenance. Technology is dominated by raw materials and the axial principle of these societies is 'traditionalism' (116–17). Industrial societies are concerned with manufacturing and with the production of goods, with energy forming the foundation of production and workers and engineers playing the leading roles. The axial principle of these societies is 'economic growth' (116–17). Postindustrial societies, in contrast, centre on the production and consumption of services. Here it is the service or tertiary sector which dominates the economy and the axial principle is the 'centrality of and codification of theoretical knowledge' (116–17). Bell states that:

> the concept of 'post-industrial society' emphasizes the centrality of theoretical knowledge as the axis around which new technology, economic growth and the stratification of society will be organized. Empirically one can try to show that this axial principle is becoming more and more predominant in advanced societies. (112)

For Bell, the most important aspect of postindustrial society is people: it is a society of human interaction. The dominant occupations are in education and further education, healthcare, the arts and the provision of other recreational activities. Others have taken a broader perspective of the knowledge economy, recognising that knowledge can play an important part in economic development in all sectors of the economy. Brint (2001) for example sees the impact of knowledge in the entrepreneurial sector, in the industrialised sector and in the professional service sector. Boden and Miles (2000) stress that the knowledge economy spans both manufacturing and services, and that there is potential to innovate in both sectors.

However, in contrast to Bell's model, economies differ in the ways in which and the means by which they promote knowledge acquisition and learning, and this is closely linked with a state's embedded institutional framework. There are different kinds of institutions of learning and these shape what is learnt and how this learning takes place. These institutions include schools, colleges and universities, as well as institutions of training and retraining at the workplace and the ability to use tacit knowledge to improve work processes such as via institutions of social partnership at the workplace.

States also innovate in different ways. Hall and Soskice (2001) differentiate between models of capitalism that promote rapid innovation and those which promote incremental innovation. Radical innovation refers to 'substantial shifts in production lines, the development of entirely new goods, or major changes to the production process' while incremental innovation refers to 'continuous but small-scale improvements to existing product lines and production processes' (38–44). The authors recognise that rapid innovation is required for the fast-moving high-technology sectors that call for innovative design and rapid product development based on research such as biotechnology, semiconductors and software development (39). Incremental innovation, on the other hand, is more important for 'maintaining competitiveness in the production of capital goods such as machine tools and factory equipment, consumer durables, engines and specialized transport equipment' (39).

Again, it is the institutional configuration underpinning an economy that clearly shapes the kind of innovation that is attempted. Hall and Soskice argue that co-ordinated market economies, such as the German model, 'should be better at supporting incremental innovation' since it is in such economies that 'the workforce . . . is skilled enough to contribute to such innovations, secure enough to risk suggesting changes to products or process that might alter their job situation, and endowed with enough work autonomy to see these kinds of improvements as a dimension of their job' (39). Indeed, the institutions of co-ordinated market economies provide industrial relations systems and corporate structures and training systems which favour incremental innovation. In liberal market economies, by contrast, the institutional arrangements – short-term financial market arrangements, fluid labour markets and top-down corporate structures – are highly supportive of rapid innovation. As Hall and Soskice (2001: 40) put it, 'labor markets with few restrictions on lay-offs and high rates of labor mobility means that companies interested in developing an entirely new product line can hire in personnel with the requisite expertise, knowing that they can release them if the project proves unprofitable'.

Conclusion: convergence and diversity in postindustrial transition

These three distinct approaches to the postindustrial economy can clearly be divided into those who think that postindustrial society is transition to a predetermined end state – be it a service sector dominated economy, a society without work or a world filled with flexibly specialised firms – and those who recognise that the transition will be constrained and enabled by the underpinning institutional frameworks. This chapter concludes by highlighting the institutionalist positions in the postindustrial debate. There are different ways in which the service sector has developed and is organised; the impact of technological transformations and information technologies on production systems varies from state to state and the way different kinds of knowledge is produced and reproduced is deeply embedded in an economy's institutional framework. The different institutional configurations clearly mean different national paths of postindustrialism. What is more, within national economies, institutions vary because of historical differences or they may be operationalised in different ways. Therefore, as we have seen in the case of Italy, just as there are different institutional configurations within national economies, so there will be distinct regional trajectories of postindustrialism. This is also clearly the case in Germany for both historical and contemporary reasons. The postindustrial transformation(s) of the German economy now need to be investigated in more detail.

3

Germany's service sector economy

For many years the notion has dominated that a postindustrial economy is one with a well-developed service sector. It was anticipated that the only job growth would be in the service sector and, if states failed to achieve this, it would lead to the end of work in that society. However, not all observers of this trend assumed that there would be a uniform transition to the service sector economy. Esping-Andersen (1990) for example identified three trajectories of service sector development in postindustrial economies: the liberal model, the social democratic model and the corporatist or conservative model (see Chapter 2). The corporatist model, of which Germany is a prime example, is characterised by a reduction of industrial employment but not by a simultaneous increase in service employment. The priority in Germany has been budgetary restraint and income equality at the expense of employment growth (Iverson and Wren 1998). Instead, the response to the decline in industrial employment has been to limit access to the labour market through early retirement and long periods of education. A further typical feature of this model is that a large number of services are, in accordance with the principle of subsidiarity, traditionally provided informally or within the family. Hence the state has been reluctant to provide the kinds of service which encourage women to take up employment.

Germany has been slower than other advanced economies at developing service sector employment. It has, in a number of studies, been characterised as 'overindustrialised' (Häußermann and Siebel 1995), 'resolutely industrial' (Lash and Urry 1994) or as 'peculiar in that its "post-industrial" employment-growth is sluggish, be it in producer, social, or "fun" services' (Esping-Andersen 1990: 198). Esping-Andersen proposes:

the main prognosis for the German trajectory, then, is that Germany will remain predominantly an industrial economy, but with diminishing numbers of people involved in production, and an ever-increasing population of housewives, the young, and the elderly excluded from employment and dependent on the welfare state'. It will be a 'workless world'. (214)

High rates of unemployment in Germany have been held up to prove the end-of-work thesis (Beck 1998; Rifkin 1996). The slow growth of Germany's service sector is frequently cited as the source of its more general economic difficulties (Manow and Seils 2000).

This chapter analyses in more detail Germany's reputation as a weakly developed service sector economy. It first assesses the state of the 'underdeveloped' service sector in Germany and investigates claims that these are exaggerated. The chapter then looks at how service sector development differs regionally within Germany. Specifically, it proposes that in deindustrialised eastern Germany, where there is still high unemployment, the attitude towards service sector employment is less sceptical and there has been a rapid growth of service sector activity. It then highlights the main barriers to the expansion of the service sector economy in Germany. It is argued that these come in the form of both formal and informal institutions that hinder a rapid expansion of service employment. The formal rules of the German model act as a constraint to the expansion of low-wage service sector employment for the low skilled, and informal institutions set preferences of economic actors and block rapid change. The chapter finally offers an assessment of some recent developments that have implications for the future of the service sector economy in Germany. It argues that measures taken to expand service sector employment are, on the whole, consistent with the German model and there will be no convergence with the polarised Anglo-Saxon postindustrial model. A key development here is the setting up of ver.di, a trade union to represent service sector employees, which is now the largest trade union in Europe.

Weak service sector development

Germany has been slower than other industrialised states to create service jobs. In international comparison, Germany has a comparatively low rate of service sector employment. According to the International Labour Organisation (ILO 2001) the percentage of employment in the service sector exceeds 70 per cent in Canada, France, the USA and the UK. In

Germany, Italy and Japan, services only account for around 65 per cent of total employment. Germany is also characterised by low levels of employment overall. The employment rate for fifteen- to sixty-four-year-olds in Germany was 65.7 per cent in 2001. This is slightly above the European Union (EU) average of 63.9 per cent, but significantly below states such as the UK at 71.6 per cent and Denmark at 75.9 per cent (Eurostat 2002). As well as a shrinking labour force, Germany also has a rapidly ageing population (EIROnline 2003). The rate of employment among women in Germany is also low. In 2001, 58.7 per cent of women aged fourteen to sixty-four were economically active. Again, this is above the EU average of 54.8 per cent, but below the UK at 64.9 per cent and Denmark at 71.4 per cent. The failure to create new jobs in the service sector is regularly cited as the cause of Germany's high rate of unemployment which averaged 8.6 per cent in 2002 (Arbeitsamt 2003). In particular, Germany has been very slow at creating low-wage jobs, which are often regarded as entry jobs for the young and the low skilled. As a consequence, unemployment is particularly high among the under twenty-fives (9.7 per cent in 2002). This has led to discussion about how Germany is experiencing the end of work (Rifkin 1996; 1997).

Service sector employment is clearly developing at a slower rate in Germany than in other competitor states. However, some argue that the service sector gap between Anglo-Saxon states and Germany is exaggerated. The argument is that much service sector activity is not picked up by official statistics and therefore remains obscured from view. Service sector activity might seem particularly low in Germany because it is carried out within manufacturing firms rather than by being outsourced to specialised firms, though Fuchs and Schettkat (2000: 215) claim that German firms actually outsource more than American firms. A further argument is that service sector activity is not registered because it falls below the threshold for social security contributions (Dathe and Schmid 2000: 5).

Service jobs outside the regular labour market in Germany have been traditionally referred to as '630 Mark Jobs' or 'Mini Jobs' This refers to an employment contract that existed until 1998 whereby employees were allowed to work for 630DM (now 325 euros) per month and not more than nineteen hours per week. The employer was then exempt from paying into the social insurance scheme, but had to pay a low headtax for each employee. The 630DM jobs grew in many service areas such as restaurants, business cleaning, hospitals, retails but the majority worked in private households (Dathe and Schmid 2000: 41). Between 1992 and

1997 an 80 per cent rise in this kind of employment was registered and, in 1997, 5.5 million 630DM contracts were signed. This accounts for 15 per cent of the labour force. These kinds of low-wage and uninsured jobs were originally meant for students and pensioners, but in 1997 women took 90 per cent of these contacts. In 1998 the newly elected SPD–Green coalition turned the tax obligation of the employer into a social security contributions (12 per cent pension and 10 per cent health insurance) and the employees have to contribute 7.5 per cent to the pensions scheme. The new regulation was intended to stall the increasing substitutions of full-time work with 630DM contracts. Service sector employment is also obscured by the use of publicly funded work creation schemes (Arbeits-beschaffungsmassnahmen or ABM) in eastern Germany and the growth of informal economic activity. It is estimated that goods and services to the value of 370 billion euros are produced on the so-called 'black' or shadow economy; in the last two and a half decades the size of informal economic activity, measured against total economic activity, has grown from 6 to 16 per cent (Meyer-Timpe *et al.* 2003); and 1 million household employ persons illegally and without formal regulation or contracts (Dathe and Schmid 2000: 41).

Regionally differentiated service sector development

Service sector employment has expanded significantly in Germany since the beginning of the 1990s when many negative accounts of Germany's postindustrial development were written. Across the whole of Germany the proportion of employment in the service sector rose from 59.2 per cent to 68.1 per cent (roughly 9 percentage points) between 1991 and 2000 (Statistisches Bundesamt 2001). However the growth of the service sector during the 1990s has not been a uniform phenomenon. The extent and rate of growth differs immensely across Germany and there are some significant regional trends which need to be highlighted.

The regions with the lowest levels of employment in the service sector are Baden-Württemberg (61.5 per cent) and Bayern (64.7 per cent). Significantly, while service sector employment is comparatively low, these regions also have the lowest rates of unemployment in the whole of Germany (5.2 per cent and 5.0 per cent respectively). The low level of service sector activity might be explained by the fact that these are regions traditionally characterised by Herrigel (1996) as Germany's decentralised industrial districts. In such regions employment industry remains high because they have been able to adapt well to the challenges of technological transformation (see Chapter 4). In other regions of western Germany levels of service employment vary. In the regions such as Nordrhein-Westfalen and Niedersachsen, which Herrigel (1996) classified as part of the autarkic industrial mode, service sector employment is around the national average of 68.1 per cent (69.2 per cent and 68.5 per cent respectively). These regions traditionally rely on large manufacturing firms. Service employment therefore remains closely linked to the manufacturing sector.

Service sector employment is significantly higher than the German average in the urban city states such as Hamburg (82.1 per cent) and Bremen (75.5 per cent). These Hanseatic city states have always been involved in services and trading, and manufacturing was never as prominent here as in autarkic and decentralised regions. Service employment has therefore tended always to dominate and these states are developing along unique trajectories. Hamburg, for example, has established itself as an international media centre. Unemployment in such regions is below the national average (9.3 per cent) but above the average for western Germany (7.4 per cent). However, Bremen has the highest unemployment rate in western Germany (12.9 per cent).

Dathe and Schmid (2000) identify an additional contrast between the rate of service employment in regions of western Germany. They differentiate between agglomerated and non-agglomerated areas, and argue that service sector growth is significantly higher in the former. This can be explained in two ways. Agglomerated areas, such as those around Hamburg, Köln, Stuttgart or München, tend to develop innovative milieus or networks at regional level which create a demand for high-skilled personal services in education, health, culture and tourism as well as business-related services and personal services. Also agglomerated areas experience a higher growth in personal and labour-intensive services. This is explained by the fact that female employment tends to be higher and this clearly leads to higher levels of service employment.

The other key distinction to be made is between regions of eastern and western Germany. The east has experienced extremely rapid rates of growth in the proportion of employment that is in the service sector. Between 1991 and 2000 it grew by 13 percentage points to 69.8 per cent in the east compared with 7.7 percentage points to 68.3 per cent in the west. The proportion of people employed in services in the new *Länder* also varies from 64.7 per cent in Thüringen to 70.6 per cent in Mecklenburg-Vorpommern. Notably though, high employment rates in services do not equate with low levels of unemployment overall, and the states

with the highest proportion of employment in the service sector also have
the highest levels of unemployment (14.9 per cent in Thüringen and 17.4
per cent in Mecklenburg-Vorpommern). There are clearly limits to the
potential of service sector growth to bring down unemployment in the
east which, at 17 per cent, remains over twice the rate of unemployment
in the west (7.4 per cent). These eastern regions, once socialist autarkic,
became deindustrialised following unification and there has been no
growth in employment in manufacturing since 1991 and little opportunity for business services to grow around the provision of services for
industrial firms, which accounts for the low level of unemployment in the
decentralised west. Also, the development of high-skill, high-knowledge
'agglomerated areas' has been slow, although there is a development in
this direction in the south-east, which has been able to draw on its decentralised traditions. Because unemployment rates are so high in the east,
there is a low level of consumption of leisure and private services.

The key to service sector growth seems to be finding a particular area
of service specialism. Some of the regions which are experiencing the
worst unemployment problems are trying to establish themselves a niche
as service providers for visitors to the region. For example, the rural
north-eastern *Land* Mecklenburg-Vorpommern, which has one of the
highest unemployment rates in unified Germany, is looking at ways to
promote itself as a lighthouse region in the area of leisure, sport and
culture (Schmid and Müller 2001).

Recent debates in Germany have recognised the fact that if unemployment is to be tackled it will be necessary to expand the service economy,
particularly low-wage jobs (Bach and Schupp 2003). It has also been
acknowledged that rather than keeping people out of the labour market
to reduce unemployment rates, expanding overall employment levels will
create a demand for services and a demand for new jobs. However, there
are a number of formal and informal institutional constraints which
render a rapid expansion of a service sector economy difficult.

Formal constraints to service sector growth

With few exceptions, the German economy has always focused more
on industrial production than on services. An institutional framework
was constructed to promote industrial production and protect full-time,
lifelong industrial employment for males of working age. While these
institutions were optimal for the industrial age, they cannot easily be

transferred to services sector, and a number of accounts of Germany's failure to create new service sector jobs, and low-wage service sector jobs in particular, focus on the barriers created by the formal institutional framework of the German model. The German model, it is argued, was constructed to support and protect the institutions of industrial work and society, but it is detrimental to the creation of jobs in the service sector.

There are a number of factors which contribute to such claims. German workers are legally protected against unfair dismissal so as to prevent a hire-and-fire culture. Workers can only be dismissed on the grounds of extremely weak economic conditions or because of the poor performance of an employee. In the former case, the rule has been that more recently recruited staff will be dismissed before longer-serving employees. Firms are obliged to pay compensation for dismissed employees, though small firms with fewer than five employees are exempt from this. Dismissal legislation means that employers are more likely to invest in retraining for staff in long-term working relationships and these employees will, in turn be more likely and able to contribute to the economic success of the firm. However, there is evidence that when the skills of older employees become redundant, workers have been moved into early retirement schemes instead of being retrained (Esping-Andersen 1999). There has also been an increase in the use of the dismissal legislation to compensate dismissed staff generously, rather than protecting their jobs (Schmid 2003). There is little evidence that dismissal legislation causes high unemployment. Rather, in the German system firms are more likely to adjust working hours than sack employees in times of economic hardship (Fuchs and Schettkat 2000). However, there is evidence that strong dismissal legislation acts as a barrier to new appointments as it means employers are committed to taking a worker on permanently from the start. In addition, high levels of regulation and protection make it particularly hard for young people, women, low-skilled and the older long-term unemployed to enter employment (Schmid 2003).

Institutions of social partnership such as works councils, the representation of labour on management boards, and collective wage bargaining act as barriers to the creation of new employment as they act to protect the rights and position of existing employees, or 'insiders', to the detriment of 'outsiders' who are trying to enter the labour market. For example, works councils are consulted on key issues such as dismissals and changes to working times, and this helps to protect existing employees, but does little to create new jobs. In a similar way, trade union involvement in instituting collective bargaining leads to wages being set at high

levels. It is possible to sustain high wages in the industrial sector where
productivity levels are high. But it is argued that high wages act as a barrier to the creation of service employment, which is less productive. It
certainly acts as a barrier to the creation of low-wage starter jobs for the
young or low skilled (Manow and Seils 2000).

Where service sector employment has developed, the coverage of institutions of social partnership, such as collective bargaining, has been thin-
ner than in the industrial sector. The exceptions are in public services
which have always been well protected. There is also evidence that collective wage bargaining is being made more flexible, despite resistance from
trade unions. This is being done in two ways: there is a trend towards
agreeing wages at the level of the firm rather than for a whole industry;
and there is increasing use of opening clauses in collective agreements
which entitle employers to abandon the conditions of the wage agreement if the economic conditions in the industry worsen. These two variations of the conventional institutions of collective bargaining are being
used in the east (see Chapter 4). These developments are even starting
to affect public service as so many authorities are bankrupt and this has
led to public sector employers abandoning collective wage agreements.
For example, in 2002 the SPD–PDS (Social Democratic Party–Party of
Democratic Socialism) coalition in the bankrupt city of Berlin abandoned
a wage agreement for its public sector workers. It was looking for ways to
cut its annual salaries budget from the current level of 7.3 billion euros
(on a tax income of just 8 billion euros) and offered the trade unions a
deal which entailed wage cuts in return for cuts in working hours and
guarantees that levels of employment would be maintained. The employers' proposal was rejected by unions and the alternative enforced outcome
entailed redundancies, increases in working hours and cutting the pay of
civil servants.

The cost of creating new jobs is also high because of the contributions to
the social security and health system that employers are obliged to pay. The
corporatist German welfare state is funded by contributions from employees and employers. The only exception is that civil servants are not required
to make any contributions to the social security system. The higher the
level of unemployment, the higher these contributions need to be in order
to fund welfare payments; the smaller the number employed, the higher
the employers' and employees' contributions are per worker. Taxes on
wages and social security contributions have risen from about 25 per cent
of gross wages in 1960 to 45 per cent in 2002. In the same period unemployment rose from 270,000 to 4.6 million (Meyer-Timpe *et al.* 2003).

These contributions sustain a German welfare state that provides a substantial level of protection for the unemployed and the sick. This high level of protection is said, in turn, to act as a further barrier to the creation of service sector employment, especially among the low skilled and the low paid. It is claimed that welfare payments are too high for there to be an incentive on the part of the unemployed to move from benefits to low-wage employment. It is argued that either wages need to be set at a high level in order to make work worthwhile, or benefits need to be made lower in order to reduce the incentive of staying on benefits. However, evidence suggests that the level of benefit does not affect the rates of employment, but long durations of entitlement do (Fuchs and Schettkat 2000: 230). The priority, then, should be to speed up the transition from welfare to work which has, in Germany, been notoriously slow. Indeed, in recent years the institutions which manage unemployment funds in Germany have been criticised for not doing enough to encourage the unemployed to move from welfare to work. It has been argued that the Federal Employment Office (Bundesanstalt für Arbeit), a federal institution which deals with unemployment benefit and co-ordinates local unemployment offices, and local Employment Offices (Arbeitsämter) themselves have been administrating or managing unemployment in a bureaucratic way rather concentrating on job placements. In January 2002 the Bundesanstalt für Arbeit was strongly criticised following a scandal that revealed that it had manipulated its figures on how many people it had moved successfully into employment: only 30 per cent of the successes it claimed were correct. This event triggered a reform process and the administration was taken over by Florian Gerster (formerly the SPD minister president of Rheinland Pfalz). He pledged to improve accountability, and reduce the bureaucracy of the institution (and its 90,000 staff) in order to improve the efficiency of placing the unemployed in work.

A final institutional barrier to expanding service sector employment is that the German welfare state has traditionally relied on male workers to be the breadwinners and has encouraged women to provide unpaid, informal caring services in the household. As Esping-Andersen has recently argued (1999: 114), households become key institutions within the postindustrial economy. They will have an influence on what kind of employment will grow and how much service employment will emerge. The development of the service sector, he argues, is threatened by household self-servicing. Self-servicing in households means that there is lower demand for many kinds of service sector activity, such as childcare or private household services. Evidence from states such as the UK or Denmark suggests that high levels of female employment create a demand for these services and lead to an expansion of employment rates overall (Esping-Andersen 1999; 2002). Therefore, states with high levels of female employment also tend to have high levels of service employment growth and low levels of unemployment.

As a conservative or corporatist welfare state Germany has traditionally promoted male employment and has kept female employment low. Instead, women have been encouraged to stay at home and provide caring services for children or other dependants, relying on men or the state for an income and access to social rights. For example, in the past it was accepted that female carers who could not rely on a male breadwinner to support them were entitled to social assistance without the obligation to seek work. Moreover, mothers have traditionally been exempt from the work obligations that social assistance benefit entails. Social assistance recipients traditionally have not been obliged to accept a work offer if having to work would endanger the rearing of children in a family or if the claimant has responsibility for the running of a household or the care of dependants (Annesley 2002; OECD 1996: 163–4; Voges et al. 2001: 78).

The GDR was, of course, different. This was a socialist adult worker state which promoted the right and duty for all citizens – male and female – to work. Unification shifted the model to the male breadwinner model, and employment rates in the east have fallen and unemployment rates among women have risen. The desire among women in the east to work remains high, and rates of employment are higher in the east than in the west.

What can be done about the barriers to creating service employment and the resultant unemployment in regulated economies such as Germany? The Eurosclerosis thesis states that Germany, and other continental European labour markets, are characterised by too much welfare, too much wage equality, too much institutional rigidity and excessive labour costs (Esping-Andersen and Regini 2000). Proponents of this argument cite the experiences of the UK and the USA as evidence that labour markets with low levels of regulation are more flexible and are better at creating new service sector employment than more regulated European economies. In order to create employment, regulated economies should therefore undergo wholesale deregulation: dismissal legislation should be slackened; employee participation at the workplace should be abandoned; wages should be determined by markets; non-wage labour costs should be drastically lowered; and welfare entitlement should be reduced and lowered.

However, the argument that jobs can be created through wholesale labour market deregulation is being contested increasingly. Esping-Andersen and Regini (2000) find no evidence of a direct causal link between labour market regulation and mass unemployment. Instead, it seems that high levels of labour market regulation affect the structure of unemployment if it favours insiders at the expense of outsiders such as the young, the low skilled and women. It therefore makes no sense to use wholesale labour market deregulation to tackle unemployment and create jobs. Rather, the structural rigidities of European labour markets are best addressed through carefully targeted measures appropriate to a particular state. The uniqueness of national institutions means that there are different inbuilt methods of creating flexibility. Moreover, Esping-Andersen and Regini (2000) argue that in order to come up with durable and stable solutions to the problems of mass unemployment, these should be negotiated with social partners.

A wholesale deregulation of the German labour market would not be an appropriate way to create new employment and tackle mass unemployment. It would also not be possible to carry out such proposals because the economic culture promotes gradual, consensual developments rather than radical reforms. There is no desire for a Thatcher-style deregulatory revolution of the labour market in Germany.

Informal constraints and the importance of industrial employment

It hard to expand the service sector because of the formal institutions of the German model. The informal institutions, or cultural norms which support this model act as an additional barrier. As Baethges (2001) rightly point out, Germany developed as a purely industrial nation whereas other nations, such as the UK, experienced a parallel development of industry and services. Germany concentrated solely on industry and there developed a strong cultural attachment to the institutions of industrial employment. The potential collapse of these institutions is perceived as a major threat to the stability and cohesion of the German economy and society. By the end of the 1970s and beginning of the 1980s concerns were expressed about the decreasing significance of the German work ethic and the ascendancy of postmaterialist values which valued leisure over work (Adagh 1991: 138–41; Inglehart 1977). Industrial employment is closely associated with German identity and it is also used as an indicator of economic and political stability.

The importance of industrial work in Germany has deep roots. Campbell (1989) argues that the Germans' strong historical attachment to work and a strong work ethic can be traced back to the Protestant Reformation in Germany and Switzerland. She writes (Campbell 1989: 8) that 'Luther, Zwingli, and Calvin all proclaimed work's value as a safeguard against idleness and sin and deemed pursuit of a calling as a major expression of faith, a form of worship in no way inferior to prayer'. The German enlightenment and idealist tradition reinforced the belief that work paves the way to self-fulfilment and offers a purpose for human existence. As Pankoke (1993) notes, this ideal found its realisation in the industrial age when work became equated with full-time, life-long employment. He argues, 'the connection between industrial expansion as a sign of modernity and the normative status of a work-centred lifestyle has been particularly important for Germany' (6). Moreover, in the post-1945 period industrialism and industrial employment played key roles in the reconstruction of economies and identities of the FRG and the GDR (Pankoke 1993).

In the GDR, industrial employment was a central economic and cultural pillar. As Wilson (1993: 142) notes 'the GDR guaranteed a right to work for all adult citizens which was matched by the responsibility to work for most citizens – men and women'. This right and responsibility to work meant that all citizens were guaranteed social rights. The GDR's equivalent of social security was confined to the long-term sick, pensioners and disabled people, while medical treatment was free. In addition, there was full childcare provision for all children.

Industrial work was of equal significance to the post-1945 reconstruction of the FRG. Industrial employment, that is full-time, lifelong employment underpinned by vocational training, developed as the model of *Erwerbsarbeit* or 'meaningful employment'. In contrast to the GDR, however, access to institutions of industrial work in the FRG was limited to the male population. Rather than providing state welfare by means of universal social rights, as in the GDR, welfare in the corporatist welfare state of West Germany was managed according to the principle of subsidiarity. This means that welfare should be provided at the level closest to the family. This model of welfare foresaw that men would be the family breadwinners while women would have informal caring roles in the home. Demand for labour in West Germany was met not by giving women access to institutions of industrial employment but by recruiting *Gastarbeiter* (guest workers).

For these reasons industrial employment is seen as a stable and superior form of work, and service employment is looked down upon. As

Baethges (2001: 32) bluntly, but rightly, puts it, 'die Deutschen wollen nicht dienen' (Germans do not want to serve). Since the institutions of industrial employment are so culturally embedded, it is hard to transform them. The model of industrial employment was a robust one which provided for economic success and a high degree of social justice. This positive experience with the industrial era means that the Germans are reluctant to give it up. The development of *geringfügige Arbeit* or marginal jobs such as part-time, service sector, personal services, home-working or the secondary labour market are perceived as a threat to the institutions of meaningful industrial employment or *Erwerbsarbeit* and any expansion of inferior forms of employment are constantly resisted. Lafontaine and Müller (1998: 337) argue that: 'the value of work, and of meaningful work in particular, should not be underestimated. Personal life chances depend to a large extent on meaningful employment . . . A democratic society must therefore help guarantee its members the right to meaningful employment'. Moreover, the reluctance to deviate from the model of meaningful industrial employment is exacerbated by the fact that there is no clear, robust or secure postindustrial order to replace the industrial order. The new order is diverse and differentiated. It is unlikely, therefore, that a coherent and compact postindustrial German model will be able to develop. There is little desire in Germany to fight to replace the existing institutional order with an insecure and uncertain one which might lead to instability and an polarised society of 'haves' and 'have nots'. The ideal is that Germany's postindustrial economy should be regulated in the same way as the former industrial order.

However, the formal institutions which act as a barrier to service sector growth in German model are less well entrenched in the east than in the west and this could, in part, explain the rapid growth of service employment in the new *Länder*. It could also facilitate more rapid growth in the future if difference continues. Wages are lower in the east than in the west, despite the commitment on the part of trade unions to equalise wages between the old and new *Länder* which was never fully realised. Also, collective bargaining is less well institutionalised and, where such agreements do exist in services, they are often at firm level rather than at industry level or they are undercut by employers who introduce opening clauses which state that employees can be paid at a lower level if the economic circumstances take a turn for the worse.

Although such developments undermine the ethos of the German model of industrial relations and are strongly resisted by the trade unions, they have become commonplace and reasonably uncontroversial in the new *Länder*. Unification destroyed the whole set of formal institutions of the GDR and replaced it with an unfamiliar set of west German institutions. The cultural attachment of east Germans to the institutions of the German model is weaker. However, what remained in the new *Länder* was a strong desire – significantly among both men and women – to be economically active. In other words, the desire to work is still there, but the adherence to industrial employment and its associated institutions is not. East Germans are less 'precious' about what kind of employment they take and there is less resistance to service employment in the east than in the west. The employment rate among women in the eastern *Länder* remains high, which could lead to high levels of service sector employment.

Despite a uniform German model, it becomes clear that service sector development in Germany is not uniform but will be regionally differentiated. This regional differentiation will depend on the industrial trajectories which preceded it, and on how good the regions are at developing either agglomerated areas of high-skill, high-knowledge business services, the level of female employment or the demand for local leisure, consumer and private services. The paths taken will vary on account of the fact that institutions are adapted and operationalised to suit regional circumstances. Some formal rules will be adapted to suit informal institutional arrangements, and some institutional rules may be played out differently to suit different *Länder*, cities or political interests.

Expanding the service sector

Despite some growth in service sector employment during the 1990s, it has not been enough to compensate for the loss of jobs in manufacturing and the expansion of the labour force and, consequently, unemployment has risen. During the 1990s mild and incremental attempts at reducing unemployment and expanding areas of new employment have been made both by the Christlich Demokratische Union-Freie Demokratische Partei (Christian Democratic Union-Free Democratic Party, CDU-FDP) coalition under Kohl and the SPD–Green coalition under Schröder. For example, Kohl implemented some deregulatory reforms of the labour market such as allowing more freedom to issue fixed term contracts and reducing sickness benefit from 100 per cent to 80 per cent of earnings. In its first term in office most of the SPD–Green government's policies were re-regulatory. In 1998 they reinstated entitlement to sickness benefit to 100 per cent and changed legislation on 630DM jobs so that they became liable to pay social insurance contributions. It even introduced legislation to bring prostitutes into standard employment by issuing them with employment contracts (Holm 2002). To tackle the issue of unemployment the government convened a new tripartite Alliance for Jobs (Bündnis für Arbeit) which brought together employers' organisations, trade unions and ministries to discuss the problems of the German labour market. These talks failed to reach any conclusion or have any significant impact on unemployment levels (Timmins 2000). Some measures had been introduced to address these issues in the first term in office, but only as pilots. For example, in 2001 an active labour market policy called Job-AQTIV was passed which aimed to increase the speed at which the unemployed are moved to the labour market. In Rheinland Pfalz, some schemes have been introduced to target in-work benefits at claimants in order to make it worthwhile to leave social assistance for employment. One such model – the Mainzer Modell – has now been extended into a national project, supporting in particular those on low incomes.

In its first term in office, the Schröder government was not successful at tackling unemployment which grew to over 4 million in spring and summer 2002. This was significant because the 4 million figure is a psychologically significant marker which indicates a real crisis. Moreover, the government's failure to tackle unemployment threatened to jeopardise their chances of re-election in September 2002. Schröder had, after all, stated that if his government failed to cut unemployment in its first term, then it did not deserve to be re-elected.

The final section of this chapter reviews some of the recent measures that have been taken to tackle unemployment and increase service sector employment in Germany. These include the proposals made by the Hartz Commission in 2002, by Schröder's controversial Agenda 2010 in 2003 and the recent trend towards actively encouraging women to enter the labour market. It then assesses the importance – actual and potential – of the large service sector trade union, ver.di, which was established in 2001. It seems that there is a clear desire to expand service employment in Germany but that there is also a clear priority to bring this into the institutional framework of the German model so that the German service economy does not become as polarised as that of the UK or the USA.

Hartz and Agenda 2010

Having failed to fulfil his promise of bringing down unemployment, Schröder sought an alternative strategy to secure his re-election in September 2002. In the summer of that year Schröder set up a commission to investigate ways of tacking unemployment and expanding employment, and promised to implement its recommendations fully if re-elected. The Hartz Commission – so called because it was headed by Dr Peter Hartz, personnel director of Volkswagen – was made up of fifteen representatives of business and trade unions and government (Table 3.1) and, as such, it was conducted along the lines of the consensual, co-ordinated approach to economic policy-making which characterises the German model. There were clear advantages of delegating the issue of unemployment and labour reform to a commission. Firstly, by means of a commission, Schröder was able to both distance himself from the problem and delegate responsibility of the solution to the specialist commission. Secondly, by promising to implement 'one-by-one' the consensus based recommendations of the commission, the re-elected government would not have to take responsibility for what might be unpopular or un-social democratic reforms.

The outcome of the commission negotiations was published on 16 August 2002 in the report *Moderne Dienstleistungen am Arbeitsmarkt* (Modern Services in the Labour Market). Following the narrow re-election

Table 3.1   **Members of the Hartz Commission**

Dr Peter Hartz	Volkswagen AG
Isolde Kunkel-Weber	ver.di trade union
Norbert Bensel	DaimlerChrysler Services AG
Dr Jobst Fiedler	Roland Berger Strategy Consultants
Peter Gasse	IG Metall trade union (Nordrhein-Westfalen)
Prof. Dr Werner Jann	Potsdam University
Dr Peter Kraljic	McKinsey & Company, Düsseldorf
Klaus Luft	Market Access for Technology Services GmbH
Harald Schartau	Minister for Employment for the Nordrhein-Westfalen
Wilhelm Schickler	Employment Office for the State of Hessen
Hanns-Eberhard Schleyer	Umbrella Organisation for German Skilled Trades
Prof. Dr Günther Schmid	Social Science Research Center, Berlin
Wolfgang Tiefensee	Major of Leipzig
Eggert Voscherau	BASF AG
Heinz Fischer	Deutsche Bank AG

of a SPD–Green coalition in September 2002, the commission's proposals were converted into legislation and have been further backed up by a second package of measures – Agenda 2010 – proposed by Schröder in summer 2003. The proposals are wide-ranging and imply a radical change to the German labour market and to the way unemployment is managed. The main aims of the reforms are to increase the speed at which the unemployed find work. This is done by creating new institutions to help the unemployed find jobs and at the same time reducing the bureaucracy of unemployment in Germany. Also, some measures have been introduced to make formal low-paid work more attractive and to oblige the unemployed to take such work.

The speed at which the unemployed find work should be increased by creating a new set of institutions and services which offer advice, care and financial support services for the unemployed. The present Employment Offices (Arbeitsämter) have been transformed to 'JobCenters'. These will promote a more individual or case by case approach to placing the unemployed in jobs. The new JobCenters will prioritise finding jobs for the unemployed with families or other caring responsibilities, the young and the long-term unemployed. The duration of unemployment should also be reduced by the creation of employment agencies called Personnel Service Agencies (PersonalServiceAgentur, or PSAs). These are independent private agencies which will advertise jobs to the unemployed. The unemployed will be expected to apply for a PSA job and will be expected to take jobs offered to them. Once a job has been accepted, the employee will be paid at the rate of unemployment benefit for a trial period and then will be paid at a rate determined by a wage agreement if the employee is taken on into normal work contract. It is intended that PSAs will provide a source of low-wage labour for firms.

The Hartz reforms introduced a new set of rules concerning what can be expected of the unemployed. These new expectations concern mobility or the location of a job, the financial conditions and what kind of work they are expected to accept. For example, young, single job-seekers will be expected to be more flexible and mobile than those with families and claimants without families will now be expected to accept employment in any part of Germany. Also, the unemployed are now expected to register with the JobCenter as soon as they have been made unemployed and, if they are offered a reasonable job with a PSA, they are obliged to take it otherwise they will have their benefits cut. The burden is also now on the job-seeker to prove that he or she cannot accept a job. The period of entitlement to unemployment benefit is being cut. It will be limited to twelve months to all workers except those over the age of fifty-five who can claim for up to eighteen months. After that the unemployed will only be able to claim new means-tested social assistance. This new benefit is a combination of the old unemployment assistance and social assistance. These have been merged to reduce bureaucracy and increase transparency.

There are also reforms to promote low-paid service sector employment and to bring illegal service sector employment into the mainstream. A key innovation is the Ich-AG and Familien-AG (literally: Me-plc and Family-plc). The idea is to promote self-employment by creating new limited companies for individuals or within families to encourage them to undertake economic activity legally rather than on the black market. If a person registers him or herself as a new Ich-AG, then he or she will receive a subsidy from the new Federal Office of Employment for three years. A Familien-AG works on the same principle but is extended to include family members. These new limited companies will be taxed at 10 per cent if earnings are below 25,000 euros per year. Finally, Agenda 2010 includes a reform of unfair dismissal laws to overcome the psychological threshold for new appointments. The proposal is that it will be easier to create new firms by giving them greater flexibility to appoint on short-term contracts.

These measure will put pressure on the unemployed to seek work, but there is less evidence that these measures will actually achieve much in the way of encouraging the growth of service sector employment. What is perhaps more significant in this respect are recent initiatives to encourage women to move from the home to become economically active.

Bringing women into the labour market

Recent debates in Germany since the election of the SPD–Green government in 1998 have begun to emphasise the importance of seeking to increase levels of female employment (Annesley 2002; 2003a). The development is to a large part driven by targets set at EU level, which seek to achieve rates of female employment of 60 per cent by 2010. More significantly, the shift to encourage mothers into employment has been driven by concerns about high levels of welfare spending, and social assistance spending in particular. According to the 2001 annual report on social issues, 24.2 per cent of social assistance recipients are lone parents and this is the second largest group after single people living on their own (Kanzleramt 2001: 187).

In 2001 a public debate on unemployment and levels of social assistance in Germany brought up for the first time the idea that women should be included in the work obligations associated with social assistance benefit. Schröder set off a so-called 'laziness debate' by announcing that no one has the right to live off welfare in Germany (Annesley 2002). Significantly, for the first time, this debate addressed the question of whether lone mothers should be included in the obligation to seek work for claimants of social assistance benefit. This debate radically alters the assumption that women with children and lone mothers are primarily mothers in the German welfare state (Annesley 2002) and marks the beginning of a shift to what Lewis (2001a; 2001b) refers to as an adult worker model welfare state.

At present, though, no specific labour market activation policies have been designed to increase employment rates among female welfare claimants. However, it seems that mothers who are social assistance claimants are increasingly likely to be considered as economically active and thus unemployed, rather than as passive social assistance recipients. Lone mothers will be included in mainstream measures which aim to decrease welfare or social assistance dependency. The direction of policy is more to improve the provision of childcare to support women in employment. Since 1996 parents in Germany have had a statutory right to childcare. But this provision does little to help working mothers as childcare is only available from the age of three and most kindergartens and schools close at lunchtime. The SPD–Green coalition agreement in 2002 predicted that in coming years 500,000 kindergarten places will become available as falling birth rates will decrease the demand for childcare places. *Länder* and local authorities will be expected to use this slack to increase provision of all-day childcare and places for the under threes. The coalition agreement also made a commitment to create an additional 10,000 all-day school places. However, the current budget difficulties – particularly at local level which funds childcare – places severe constraints on these commitments.

Changes have also been made to the provision of parenting leave (*Erziehungsurlaub*), which used to be granted for two years and needed to be taken at one time. Since January 2001 parenting leave has been change to parenting time (*Erziehungszeit*) and it no longer needs to be taken in one single block; the third year can be taken at any time up to the child's eighth year. In two-parent families, parents can take time off together. This links in to a broader initiative from the ministry responsible for families, called *Mehr Spielraum für Väter* (literally: more playtime for fathers), which aims to promote men's role in childrearing. Parenting allowance (*Erziehungsgeld*) of 307 euros per month is paid to parents in the first two years but if this is only claimed for one year then the payment is 460 euros, offering an incentive to return to work after one year. Finally, parents now have the right to work part-time hours if their workplace employs more than fifteen employees.

Ver.di: a trade union for service sector workers

The proposals of Hartz and Agenda 2010 met with a high degree of opposition from the left within the SPD and from trade unions. They were concerned about the reduction of welfare entitlement and the creation of unprotected, low-wage service sector jobs. The priority amongst trade unions has been for the emerging service sector to be as well protected and regulated as industrial employment, and to resist any trend towards a polarised situation of privileged professional knowledge workers on the one hand and exploited unprotected low-wage workers on the other.

Trade unions have struggled to come up with constructive solutions to the problems of the German labour market and the challenges of the emerging postindustrial era which is increasingly diverse and complex. Given declining membership and funds, they tend to defend their existing interests at the expense of forging creative solutions. At the same time, trade unionists themselves realise that if their unions do not transform themselves to address the new postindustrial paradigm and its employees, then they will suffer further losses in membership and influence (Huber 1999). Trade unions in Germany have begun to orient themselves to the new postindustrial paradigm. A major development was the unification in March 2001 of five existing service sector unions to form ver.di (Table 3.2), the Vereinte Dienstleistungsgewerkschaft (Unified Service Sector Union). With over 2.7 million members, ver.di is now the largest union in Europe.

The purpose of the merger was to combine resources, offer a proactive response to the changing shape of the political economy and contemporary labour markets and to offer a response to problems such as unemployment (Keller 1999: 611). It was thought to be the start of a new direction in German industrial relations. Above all it demonstrated clearly that efforts were being made to adapt the trade union landscape to suit the new conditions and to minimise the risk that postindustrial Germany would become a deregulated, wage agreement free, codetermination free and trade union free zone. In his speech at the ver.di founding

Table 3.2   Ver.di and its constituent unions

Ver.di: Vereinte Dienstleistungsgesellschaft (Unified Service Sector Union)
DAG: Deutsche Angestelltengewerkschaft (German Union of Salaried
     Employees)
DPG: Deutsche Postgewerkschaft (German Postal Workers Union)
hbv: Gewerkschaft Handel, Banken und Versicherung (Commerce, Banking and
     Insurance Union)
IG Medien: Media Union
ÖTV: Gewerkschaft Öffentliche Dienste, Transport und Verkehr (Union for
     Public Service, Transport and Communication)

---

conference on 20 March 2001, the leader of the new trade union, Frank
Bsirske, emphasised the need for the trade union to combine the old traditions and aims of the labour movement with the new challenges and
demands of the new labour market. As Mai (1999: 589) put it:

> founding a new [service sector] union will prove that trade unions are not a
> species of dinosaur that has died out with the industrial age. It can be
> demonstrated that unions are able to adapt and respond to the challenges of
> the information and service economy and society. We want to modernise
> and find ways of developing solidarity in a more individualised society.

Ver.di's success depends on whether it is able to respond to the complexity of the service sector economy and its employees. In the past
unions have tended to be organised centrally and hierarchically, and
they developed to represent full-time, lifelong, male industrial workers.
This has meant that unions have been able to be coherent and solidari-
daristic in their approach. However, in the postindustrial age, unions
need to be well represented at lower levels so that members have clear
link with the union and so that the unions can respond appropriately
to the local conditions and the features of the regionally distinct postindustrial trajectories and to the different priorities of male and female
workers. Ver.di is an organisation that shows a lot of potential in both of
these regards.

Ver.di's structure is not centralised and hierarchical but as a matrix
organisation (Table 3.3). It is divided vertically, into thirteen *Fachbereiche*
(subject areas) which represent the interest areas of the five original
organisations. Horizontally, the trade union is represented at federal level,
thirteen regional units and 110 local offices. The vertical dimension of
ver.di is responsible for subject issues and the horizontal levels are responsible for political issues (Hasibether 2001: 177). A third dimension of the

Table 3.3   Ver.di: a matrix organisation

Thirteen subject areas (Fachbereiche)	Three horizontal levels
1 Financial services	1 Federal
2 Energy, water and waste management	2 Regional
3 Health and social services	3 Local
4 Social insurance	
5 Education, science and research	
6 Federal and regional government	
7 Local government	
8 Media, arts, paper and printing	
9 Telecommunications and IT	
10 Postal services and logistics	
11 Transport	
12 Retail and wholesale trade	
13 Special services	
Young, old, unemployed	

ver.di matrix represents the interests of specific membership groups such as the young, the old and the unemployed.

The ver.di matrix creates a decentralised and differentiated union structure. Ver.di will have to be successful in balancing the different horizontal and vertical dimensions to its matrix structure. There are concerns, however, that there will be insufficient coherence between the vertical and the horizontal dimensions of the organisation and that these could act independently and irresponsibly to undermine the overall coherence of the union. There are also concerns that the agreed structure is balanced in favour of the subject areas and that there is not enough representation in the lower levels of the organisation and the number of local offices is set to fall.

In the post-1945 industrial period of German trade unionism, trade unions have focused on a particular client group – industrial male workers, employed in full-time, lifelong conditions – and have come up with 'off the peg' solutions to labour market problems, such as pushing for the thirty-five hour working week. Ver.di clearly accepts that it is not possible for these industrial conditions to be reproduced in the service sector where working conditions and hours are more differentiated. A balance has to be struck between establishing ver.di as a new union which represents a new direction in trade union politics and new clientele, especially the young, women and those in new areas of economic activity on the one hand, and retaining the valued and familiar past on the other (Mai 1999: 586). Bsirske claims that the aim is not to come up with a patent recipe and dictate how its members should spend their time or organise their life, nor 'nanny' them but, rather, to create an environment where they are informed about their rights and have the support and confidence to organise their working lives in a way that suits them (Bsirske 2001a; 2001b).

Ver.di is not characteristic of the old industrial worker trade union. As an organisation which represents the service sector its members include a significant proportion of salaried workers and a high number of women. Employment in services has increased by 1.1 per cent among men and 6.6 per cent among women between 1991 and 1997 (Mai 1999: 584). The working conditions of women in service industries in Germany are poorer than those of men (Ahlers and Dorsch-Schweizer 2001). Women's issues are being taken particularly seriously, not least because over half of ver.di's members are women (Keller 1999: 20; Mai 1999: 588). Ver.di included a paragraph in its founding programme promoting the equal representation of the sexes throughout the ver.di organisation. This goal was not met when the first set of secretaries were appointed (particularly at regional and local levels) but the leadership has stated a commitment to changing this (Bsirske 2001a: 326). In addition ver.di was the first union to implement gender mainstreaming. This means that all proposals are checked to see if there are implications for women and to check that they are fair to both sexes (Ahlers and Dorsch-Schweizer 2001). Wage agreements should also be checked to consider the implications of wage agreements for men and women. Ver.di's commitment to gender politics appears to be implemented only half-heartedly. In interviews conducted with regional level trade union representatives in December 2002 and January 2003, the consensus of opinion was that gender issues were given secondary priority with the organisation (Annesley 2003b).

Verdi needs to find a balance between preserving the old members and recruiting new members and expanding into union 'blank spots' – firms not covered by works councils or collective bargaining agreements (Keller 2001b). The dilemma is that it is important to cater first and foremost for the members and the union's limited resources also make this a priority. But it is also important to try to extend the institutions of social partnership into blank spots in order to preserve and reproduce the system as a whole. There are blank spots in some sectors of the old economy, especially retail, and in new areas of economic activity, for example in call centres, design and advertising, private radio, personal services and in IT. There are also blank spots in the new *Länder* where the institutions of social partnership have not been properly implemented.

There have been campaigns by ver.di and its constituent unions to tackle these blank spots (Bsirske 2001b; Hamann 2001; Mattauch 2001; Müller, H.-P. 2001). In retail, the ver.di constituent union *hbv* ran a successful campaign to establish works councils in the drug store, Schlecker, in which mostly women worked for wages below the agreed rate and in what were criticised as being aggressive, humiliating and controlling environments. hbv formed alliances with politicians, artists and priests to bring the case to public attention and politicians 'adopted' women working in the company and threatened to cause aggravation if the women were fired. A press campaign created a great deal of support for the women. Customers boycotted the shops and the revenue in some branches fell by a third. After five months works councils were elected and wages were backpaid to bring them up to the agreed levels (Bsirske 2001b).

In the new economy ver.di has set up two projects – TIM and CONNEX – to encourage membership and the formation of works councils in the blank spots in IT, telecommunications and the media. The projects act as information points for the employees of these areas of the new economy and they have been proactive in encouraging these to set up works councils. Instead of distributing leaflets and organising meetings, it has sent email shots to all employees of specific firms in blank spots and has set up online discussion forums. These projects have been successful and some twenty firms in the new economy, such as Pixelpark in Berlin, have set up works councils. However, it is hard to recruit these workers as members (Bsirske 2001b; Hamann 2001; Mattauch 2001; Müller, H.-P. 2001).

The blank spots in the east also need to be tackled. In his speech at the founding conference of ver.di, the leader, Bsirske, identified three main problems in the new *Länder*: only every second worker is paid according to a wage agreement; high unemployment leads to heightened competition between the employees; there is wage dumping and the wages of east Germans are being undercut by people employed from the neighbouring states. He stated that ver.di is committed to addressing these issues, emphasising that the union must strive for an equalisation of wage levels between east and west, and for solidarity payments from the west to be maintained at a high level (Bsirske 2001b).

Conclusion: different service sector trajectories

In recent years in Germany, service sector employment has been growing at a significant rate, though the development has varied across the country.

The rate of growth has, however, not been fast enough to compensate for the fall of jobs in manufacturing and the growth of the labour market and, as a consequence, unemployment has remained high. The slow growth in service sector employment can be explained by the fact that the institutions of the German model promoted a certain model of regulated, secure industrial employment and the shift to service employment threatens to undermine this. The priority has been to promote wage equality.

Measures are increasingly being taken to promote employment in the service sector. This has been done in a consensual and incremental way and any signs of the creation of a low-wage service sector have met with resistance. The creation of the large service sector union, ver.di, suggests that the service sector in Germany will develop in line with the institutions of the German model and that there will be continuing resistance to the deregulated conditions of the Anglo-Saxon model. However, it seems unlikely that the union will be able to pursue a policy of wage equality across services in Germany for too much longer.

4

Germany's technological transformation

The service economy model has tended to dominate debates about postindustrialism. Yet, not all states have taken this path to the postindustrial economy and society. An alternative way of looking at the postindustrial economy is to assess the impact of technological innovations on models of capitalism and to investigate how well industrial production systems are adjusting to the demands of the new global markets. As Castells (1996) has argued, industrial economies adapt to the challenges of the information technological revolution in different ways because their institutional frameworks predispose them to particular responses. While Britain in the 1980s responded to the development and introduction of new technologies with a period of rapid industrial decline and the reduction of manufacturing employment (Gamble 1985), the West German economy successfully adapted its industrial production in a co-ordinated way (Soskice 1999) retaining high levels of employment in manufacturing. Indeed, certain regions within western Germany, such as the south-west, adapted particularly well and came to be cited as textbook examples of successful post-Fordist economies or as industrial districts with flexible specialisation (Amin 1994; Herrigel 1996; Piore and Sabel 1984; Sabel 1994).

Using the indicator of technological transformation, Germany is often seen as a postindustrial success story. This chapter investigates this claim further. It assesses Germany as an economy that has successfully undergone technological transformation and highlights the aspects of Germany's institutional framework that have facilitated this trajectory. It then considers the limitations of this approach. It looks first at the situation in the new *Länder* where developments following unification have more in common with the deindustrialisation experienced by 1980s' Britain than the technological transformation of 1980s' West Germany. It argues that both the economic conditions and the virtuous institutional configuration that facilitated West Germany's transition have never existed in the same way in the east and that is has therefore developed in a different way. It then looks at evidence which suggests that the success of the west German regions started to reach it limits by the mid-1990s. The chapter finishes by looking at recent reforms of one particular institutions of the German model – works councils – that has facilitated the technological transformation path of postindustrial development to see how these are adapting with the changing postindustrial paradigm.

Technological transformation and the institutions of the German model

The German economy is regularly cited as a model of industrial economy that has successfully integrated technological innovations into existing production methods to adapt them to a new technological paradigm (Harding and Paterson 2000; Soskice 1999). Castells (1996) identifies Germany as an example of the Industrial Production Model of the postindustrial economy. In this model, manufacturing activities have been restructured to adapt to the new sociotechnical paradigm, rather than being rapidly scaled down. The share of manufacturing employment remains at a high level: around one-quarter of the labour force (Castells 1996: 229–30). Indeed, rates of employment in manufacturing in Germany have remained high. There is evidence that they fell during the 1980s and 1990s but the rate of decline was clearly slower that in other advanced industrial states. Between 1980 and 2000, manufacturing employment fell from approximately 34 to 24 per cent. This compares with a decline from 25 to 21 per cent in Japan and from 28 to 17 per cent in the UK (ILO 2001). Figures from the German statistical office suggest that an even higher proportion of Germans work in industrial production. According to their statistics, the proportion of the labour force in Germany working in production industries was 29.4 per cent in 2000 (Statistisches Bundesamt 2001).

Germany's ability to transform its manufacturing sector and retain high levels of employment can be explained by the formal and informal institutions of the German model which became embedded in the post-1945 period. The virtuous effect of a set of key institutions meant that industrial production could be transformed in a long-term, incremental and consensual manner rather than by rapidly abandoning industrial production and industrial employment in favour of a polarised service sector economy. These are trade unions, collective wage bargaining, code-termination and training.

In the post-1945 period German trade unions reorganised themselves along the principle of one union for each industry. For example, IG Metall represented workers employed in the metalworking industry. Collectively most trade unions were members of an umbrella organisation – the Deutscher Gewerkschaftsbund (German Trade Union Federation – DGB) (Schneider 1989). This structure prevented competition and division within the labour movement and put trade unions in a strong bargaining position. From this position of strength trade unions successfully campaigned for high wages and the reduction of working hours. Since 1948, trade unions and employers' organisations have had the right to independently negotiate wage levels and, during the post-1945 period, wage agreements became centralised and uniform. Social partners agreed an agreement for a whole industry (*Flächentarifvertrag*) which stated a uniform minimum for wages, working hours, holidays and other terms and conditions of employment. Trade unions had the leverage in institutions of social partnership to negotiate high wages for their members in that industry. However, during periods of recession and economic hardship, trade unions were also willing to make moderate wage demands in return for reduced working hours or promises of higher rewards in the future. As well as wage bargaining, trade unions actively campaigned for improvements in democracy at the workplace and this led to the introduction and extension of two important institutions of social partnership.

Codetermination (*Mitbestimmung*) is facilitated through two institutions at the firm level: in works councils and through labour representation on supervisory boards. Labour gained legal rights to be represented by works councils through Paragraph 1 of the Works Constitutions Act (Betriebsverfassungsgesetz, or BetrVG) of 1972. This gives employees the right to elect works councils if they work in firms with more than five permanent employees over the age of eighteen (Kittner 1997: 586–7). Works councils have participation rights, that is, the right to be informed and consulted by management, as well as codetermination rights or 'the right to veto management decisions in areas such as the classification and reclassification of workers, working time arrangements, overtime, and to a more limited extent, recruitment and dismissal' (Auer 1997: 19). Works councils are considered to be important from the perspective of both economic efficiency and equity, and they make a substantial contribution to economic success in various ways. Works councils collect information on the preferences of workers. This means that workers can express their concerns about workplace conditions and production rather than leaving the firm. Works councils can encourage good morale, lower labour turnover and this, in turn, facilitates long-term corporate strategy and helps maximise competitiveness and productivity. More generally, they can be used to draw on the expertise of labour which, in turn, aids successful restructuring processes. Also, such institutions of social partnership are understood to breed trust and create 'social capital' that benefits not only individual employees but also, in a more intangible way, society as a whole (Bertelsmann Stiftung and Hans-Böckler Stiftung 1998). On the other hand, works councils slow down the decision-making process of firms. Business leaders in Germany complain that these institutions are expensive, bureaucratic and detrimental to job creation. Some economic research even claims that works councils bring few economic advantages. Economists who are opposed to these institutions argue that there are other ways of including labour in decision-making processes (teamwork) and that the absence of works councils does not necessarily denote an absence of labour consultation and participation (Addison *et al.* 2002: 25–6).

The second area in which labour gained the legal right to codetermination is by being represented on supervisory boards (*Aufsichtsrat*). This right was first awarded to labour in the coal and steel industries in 1952 (Kittner 1997: 1102–3). Here, labour was awarded 'parity of seats on the supervisory board and the appointment of a worker director, responsible for social welfare matters and personal matters to the management board' which is responsible for day-to-day running operations (Auer 1997: 17). Rights of codetermination were extended to other industries in a more limited way in 1952 in the BetrVG (Works Constitution Act). According to this Act, 'only a third of the members of the supervisory board of all joint-stock companies and of all limited liability companies with more than five hundred employees had to directly elect representative of the work force' (Auer 1997: 17). A fuller version of codetermination was introduced in 1976 to all joint-stock companies through the Codetermination Law (Mitbestimmungsgesetz). This law gives labour the right to codetermination on the supervisory board in joint-stock companies with over 2,000 employees. There is parity between shareholder and employee representatives of the supervisory boards. However, the chair of the board, who always represents the shareholders, holds the casting vote if there is no majority (Kittner 1997: 1080). As Auer (1997: 18) points out, the institutions of codetermination at the supervisory board level are 'an important means for unions to gain access to information and to influence board decision making, [however], the decisions supervisory boards make are often regarded as relatively unimportant'.

The transformation of industrial production was also facilitated by the fact that the German model promoted secure employment in a high-skill and high-wage economy. Industrial workers were trained as specialists to a high level and this, in turn, promoted superior levels of productivity. The system of research and development in Germany promoted incremental innovation in manufacturing rather than rapid innovation in new areas of economic activity. Because employees are highly skilled, they are able (and inclined) to use their expertise and tacit knowledge, and get involved in the implementation of innovations into production (see Chapter 5). Moreover, because employees are protected from dismissal and enjoy long-term employment relationships (see Chapter 3) they are also inclined to invest their skills and tacit knowledge in the process of transforming production. Employers are less likely to invest in the skills of employees who are not committed to a firm and, similarly, employees will not be inclined to get involved in improving production processes if they are in insecure employment (see Chapter 5).

This collection of institutions has created favourable conditions for the gradual transformation of industrial production to adopt new technological innovations. They have facilitated a gradual and incremental process of technological transformation in industrial production and this has been negotiated among the social partners. These institutions also help explain why there has been no dramatic collapse of West German industrial employment. However, this unitary, formal institutional framework has had varying impacts across Germany. In order to explain the differences in the success of different regions in industrial transformation, it is necessary to look at how these institutions have operated in the regions of Germany.

Regional variations in technological transformation

West Germany shared in the post-1945 period the same industrial institutional framework and this has played a key role in the gradual technological transformation of the German industrial economy and in maintaining high levels of industrial employment. Germany, as a whole, has successfully sustained high levels of industrial employment in comparison with other industrial states. However, a more regional approach indicates that it is unwise to make generalisations. It is particularly necessary to draw distinctions between the success of the old *Länder* compared with the collapse of the new *Länder*. The technological transformation paradigm is appropriate, therefore, for western Germany, but not the new *Länder*. Industrial employment in Germany as a whole stood at 29.4 per cent of overall employment in 2000. This had fallen by 7.3 percentage points from 1991. However, in the same year, in Baden-Württemberg 36.2 per cent of employees worked in the production industry and in Bayern it was 31.6 per cent. This had fallen only marginally in the 1990s by 6.8 percentage points and 5.6 percentage points respectively. In Nordrhein-Westfalen employment in industrial production fell at a faster rate from 38.1 per cent in 1991 to 29.3 per cent in 2000 (8.8 percentage points). In city states such as Berlin and Hamburg there was much less employment in industrial production (18.6 per cent and 17.5 per cent respectively), and the rates of decline were therefore low – in both cases it fell by about 5 percentage points.

In the eastern part of Germany, employment in industry is slightly below the average for Germany as a whole (27.2 per cent) but the rate of decline between 1991 and 2000 was alarming. While in the west employment in the production industries fell by 6.8 percentage points from 36.1 to 29.3 per cent, in the east it fell by a massive 10.2 per cent from 37.4 to 27.2 per cent. In the states of Sachsen, Sachsen-Anhalt and Thüringen the drop in manufacturing employment was most dramatic. In all these states industrial employment fell by 11 or 12 percentage points from 1991 to 2000.

There is a clear relationship between the rate of destruction of manufacturing jobs and unemployment rates. Where industrial employment has collapsed rapidly, unemployment rates are high. Similarly, where these have barely fallen, unemployment is low. For example, in Bayern industrial employment fell by just 5.6 percentage points between 1991 and 2000 and unemployment in this state was 5.0 per cent in 2000. In Sachsen-Anhalt, industrial employment fell by 11.5 percentage points in the same period and unemployment in 2000 was 19.9 per cent.

Regional variations in technological transformation can be explained by the fact that coexisting industrial modes have adapted in different ways and with varying degrees of success to the challenges of the postindustrial paradigm. Herrigel (1996) divided German industrial production into the autarkic mode and the decentralised mode (see Chapter 1). The way that these adapted to the challenges of the Information Technology Revolution was illustrated by Castells (1996) (see Chapter 2).

Using Castells's typologies, it seems that the regions such as Nordrhein-Westfalen and Niedersachsen characterised by the autarkic industrial order transformed into the Industrial Production Model with which Germany is typically associated. However, the slightly more successful regions such as Baden-Württemberg, Bayern and Hessen have the older decentralised industrial tradition. Their transformation is more akin to what Castells (1996) alludes to as the Networking Model. In this model there are 'different organizational [employment] arrangements, based on networks of small and medium businesses' (230). What is distinctive about this model is the way in which these networks of SMEs have successfully adapted, through their ability to innovate rapidly to changing consumer tastes and the changing conditions within the global economy thus 'laying the ground for an interesting transition from proto-industrialism to proto-informationalism' (230).

Indeed there is evidence of this. Technological advances in global production systems since the 1970s led to a revival of the tradition of decentralised regional economies (Sabel 1989). Such regions in Germany benefited not only from the virtuous effect from the institutional framework of the German model, but were also able to draw from the old networking tradition and this enabled SMEs co-operating with each other to shift to a production system referred to as flexible specialisation. This allowed them to innovate more rapidly, and to create high-quality niche products to meet changing consumer demands. As a consequence, at the end of the 1980s, these regions were held up as the model for the future of industrial production in Germany and elsewhere. While post-Fordists assumed that the model of flexible specialisation could be applied as a new system of production to all advanced industrial economies (Amin 1994), representatives of the industrial districts school rightly recognised the fact that such virtuous sets of institutions are historically embedded and can, therefore, not be transferred (Kenny 1999; Sabel 1994).

In western Germany there is evidence of two kinds of successful technological transformation of industrial production. This success can be attributed to the institutions of the post-1945 German model and the traditions of the industrial models which date from industrialisation. The paradigm of technological transformation presupposed therefore that there is an industrial base and an embedded institutional framework which acts in a virtuous way to transform industrial production. This helps us to understand why it is that the industrial economy of the new *Länder* has not transformed in the same way. It can be argued that, despite the fact that unification entailed a wholesale transfer of the institutions and organisations of the German model, these had not become embedded as the GDR industrial base was simultaneously collapsing. The economy was, in turn, under strain because the institutional framework was placing unsustainable demands on East German industry. Furthermore, the formal institutions that had been transferred were supplemented by the tenacious informal institutions of the GDR.

The GDR was a socialist state dominated by large, state-owned, centrally run autarkic firms (*Kombinate*). One of the major tasks of unification was to transform the centrally planned, state-owned economy of the GDR into a capitalist market system. This was approached through the agency Treuhand (Trustee Office) whose task was to 'break up the monolithic state economic system by a combination of methods: returning some establishments to former owners, finding private buyers for others, transferring some to local authorities, and closing others down altogether' (Hyman 1996: 3). By the time Treuhand wound up its business in the mid-1990s there had been a large-scale destruction of the former East German economic base. Industrial production had declined by 70 per cent and there had been an almost total deindustrialisation of some parts of eastern Germany (4).

Hyman accounts for this industrial collapse by highlighting the following six problems (3–4). Treuhand's strategic objectives favoured the rapid transfer or closure of state enterprises over extended process of assistance to firms which might have enabled them to survive in the new competitive environment. The breakup of state *Kombinate* also destroyed the informal networks through which managers in the GDR evaded the inefficiencies of central planning. East German firms were affected by a loss of markets for their products. This came about through the collapse of the Soviet bloc and through the decline in domestic demand for eastern products when East Germans started to demand products from the west. The German economic union meant that East German products had to be paid for in hard currency (Deutsche Mark) which outpriced them in other eastern markets. East German firms required substantial investment to meet western standards of production and environmental control. East German management also lacked the skills – in particular marketing – required for survival in a market economy. The collapse of the GDR economy has led to a new economy in the eastern part of Germany which has come to be marked by deindustrialisation, drastically reduced levels of employment in industrial production and very high levels of unemployment.

There was not a uniform collapse of the East German economy. Certain sectors suffered more than others and, within sectors, branches were affected differently (Czada 2000; 2002). The most affected sectors were those which were export oriented and were closer to the market. Industrial firms which had been particularly involved in the production aims of the socialist state suffered major collapse in production and employment. The sectors which were more successful and suffered the fewest job losses were areas of economic activity such as telecommunications, energy, rail and post. These were not particularly affected because they were integrated with a similar state structure in the west. Also, the banking sector was successful because it tapped into a new demand for financial services. Branches such as agriculture, food, building materials and the local service sector, which provided for local and regional markets, were also successful (Czada 2000: 177).

Similarly, the recovery of the east German economy has not been uniform, although post-unification policy did aim for this. Shortly after unification, Chancellor Kohl promised that within three years there would be 'flourishing landscapes' across the whole of the east. Kohl's pledge was based on a strategy that relied almost wholly on subsidiaries of west German foreign companies investing in the new *Länder*. It also depended on the development of owner-managed SMEs (Carlin and Richthofen 1995: 4, cited in Hyman 1996: 4). There is some evidence of successful transformation of industrial production in east Germany. One frequently cited firm is Jena Optik. Also, a number of modern car plants have been set up in the east. In July 2001 BMW decided to invest in a production plant in Leipzig. However, by 1993 it became apparent that it would not be possible to uniformly transform the autarkic conditions of the west German economy to the east. Instead the approach was altered to concentrate on the preservation and promotion of core 'lighthouse' regions. This has led to the assessment that the transformed east German economy resembles 'islands of high technology within a sea of backwardness' (Hyman 1996: 4).

The most successful lighthouse regions are those which had some industrial tradition prior to the establishment of the GDR. According to Herrigel's (1996) historical analysis, the ex-GDR originally was divided equally between an agricultural north, an autarkic centre and a decentralised south. In the GDR, the whole economy was transformed into state socialist autarky. Agricultural regions were industrialised and the decentralised regions brought into the centralised command economy. Following the fall of the Berlin Wall, industrial production collapsed and the region became deindustrialised. The areas that suffered the most drastic deindustrialisation were those which were tightly locked into the autarkic and hierarchical centrally planned economy and these tended to be concentrated in the previously unindustrialised regions of the eastern part of Germany (e.g. Mecklenburg Vorpommern and Brandenburg). South-east Germany originally belonged to the decentralised tradition of German industrialism, which is characterised by networks of highly innovative SMEs. Networks of production did not survive in the GDR economy. However, there is indicative evidence that this region was not completely derailed from its decentralised trajectory, and that the decentralised tradition is being revived in the east, albeit in new east German manifestation (Bowley 1998). The south-east region seems to have been able to recover faster and seems to have been able to draw from its old decentralised tradition. Heuser and von Randow (1998) provide a number of examples of how certain areas of south-eastern Germany – Chemnitz, Leipzig, Neukirsch/Lausitz, Halle, Hoyerswerda, Dresden – are being regenerated by founding networks of interest. These networks of *gegenseitige Hilfe* (mutual assistance) are made up of firms, the state, universities, trade unions, churches and other community initiatives. It is suggested that these networks are established not for pure market economic purposes, but that they have less materialistic goals.

Imperfect institutional transfer to the east

According to Castells's (1996) typology, states which adapt to the ITR by rapidly scaling down industrial production tend to go on to find a new niche in the production and provision of services. While there is clear evidence that the proportion of people employed in the service sector in the new *Länder* has increased rapidly in the period since unification (see Chapter 3), it would be wrong to label the new *Länder* as typical of Castells's Service Economy Model. Norten-Standen argues that as a consequence of the upheavals of 1989 and the transition period of the 1990s, the ex-socialist states of eastern Europe lost both their industrial base and the industrial institutions which had developed with it. The lack of industrial baggage – industrial institutions and entrenched industrial mindsets – should allow these states to leapfrog into the postindustrial age. They can implement necessary radical change unhindered by the formal and informal institutional rigidities that frustrate innovation in west Germany (Herrigel 1997). East Germany was one of the eastern European states that lost its industrial base and industrial institutions and had the potential to leapfrog western European states into the postindustrial age.

However, its capacity to create a clean slate and leapfrog into the postindustrial age was hindered by the institutional baggage it adopted from
western Germany at the time of unification. At the time of unification the
social and economic institutions of the German model were transferred
wholesale, with few exceptions, to the new eastern *Länder*. This transfer
included organisations and institutions of social partnership such as
trade unions, collective wage bargaining and codetermination. The
impact of wholesale institutional transfer of the west German model to
the east can be illustrated by looking at how successfully organisations
and institutions of social partnership have been implemented since
1989–90.

Trade union organisations transferred to the east in three stages, which
can be characterised as irritation, infiltration and integration (Tiemann
et al. 1993: 41–2). During the phase of irritation, from 9 November 1989
to the end of 1989, the institutions and organisations of the GDR started
to be restructured and redefined. The GDR remained independent, and
the west, therefore, remained at a distance. Since there was no intention
of unifying the two German states at this time, no attempt was made on
the part of the unions to merge. The second phase – infiltration – took
place during the first few months of 1990. This phase was triggered by
Kohl's ten-point plan which proposed a confederation of the two German
states. The plan also marked the point at which the west started to influence and shape the institutions of the east. The most significant event for
the unions during this phase was at the east German trade union movement's (Freier Deutscher Gewerkschaftsbund; the Free German Trade
Union Federation or FDGB) congress from 31 January to 1 February
when the FDGB decided to detach itself from the Socialist Unity Party
(Sozialistische Einheitspartei or SED) and restructure itself according to
the model of the west German DGB and its constituent unions. The
FDGB gave up its role as a central unit of authority in the socialist state
and became, instead, an umbrella organisation with independent, individual unions affiliated to it. The affiliated unions realigned in order to
mirror the sectors of industry which they were to represent and their sister unions in the west. The third stage – integration – followed the results
of the Peoples' Chamber (Volkskammer) elections which took place on
18 March 1990. At this stage the west German legal framework as well as
social and economic institutions were transferred to the east. This gave
unions in the east the same legal mandate, role and function as those in
the west. Accordingly, works councils and supervisory boards were for the
first time elected in the east. Finally, as of 30 September 1990 the FDGB

ceased to exist. It was not merged with the DGB, rather, it was dissolved and the DGB structure was then extended to the east. To accommodate this change, the DGB amended only one aspect of its statute – Clause 3, Part 1, Paragraph 1, which had earlier restricted the geographical extent of DGB to the old *Länder*. No other concessions were made at that time. Attempts were made to implement the institutions of social partnership in the same way. In the realm of collective bargaining, a consensus emerged in the early post-*Wende* era between unions, employers and government in the west that a rapid equalisation of wage rates should be aimed for. This decision was made despite the fact that such a policy would pose major challenges for the competitiveness of the east German industry which had considerably lower productivity, longer working hours and shorter holidays. The decision to aim for rapid wage equalisation was influenced by three factors. One was that the fear of low-wage competition from the east would undermine the established, and highly valued, conditions of the west. A second concern was that with a policy of wage equalisation it would be possible to stem the economic migration of east Germans to the west. Finally, there was political pressure for the former East Germany to reach the standard of living of the west (Hyman 1996: 10). The deindustrialisation and mass unemployment which followed the *Wende* and economic recession of 1993 contributed to the failure of the policy of wage equalisation. Following the recession of 1993 a deadlock in wage negotiations between the metalworkers' trade union and employers' association was solved with two compromises. The date for realisation of wage equalisation was put forward two years to 1996 and, for the first time, *Härtefallklauseln* (hardship clauses) were permitted. These agreements allowed firms in economic difficulties to pay below the negotiated wage rate as long as a committee, which was to include union representation, had agreed. Hyman (1996: 12) proposes that this compromise was a turning point which may lead to three permanent features of east German industrial relations. Firstly, it signalled a retreat from the tripartite commitment to rapid equalisation of wage levels and working conditions. Secondly, eastern Germany has become a laboratory for the flexibilisation of collective bargaining. Thirdly, the coverage of collective wage agreements is much less encompassing in the east than in the west. There is now a well-practised phenomenon referred to as *Tarifflucht* (flight from collective agreements) whereby firms leave employers' associations in order to avoid the constraints of sectoral pay settlements, or so that they can simply undercut the negotiated rate. Hyman (1996: 12) notes that 'association officials – and . . . trade unions as well – turn a blind eye to such (illegal) practice if the survival of the company seems at stake'.

The collapse of industrial employment has also directly affected trade union membership. In the initial post-*Wende* period, west German trade unions benefited greatly from the fact that membership of the FDGB had been compulsory. This membership was transferred to the corresponding union in the west and trade union membership in eastern Germany remained high. However, the destruction of industrial employment in the east destroyed trade union membership with it. Trade unions then suffered from a reduction of funds and had fewer resources with which they were expected to cover a greater range of problems and scenarios. Many of their efforts were directed at offering training to east German employees about the legal framework.

Institutions of social partnership – works councils and labour representation on supervisory boards – were set up in the early stages of post-*Wende* eastern Germany. A successful operationalisation of the organisations and institutions of the German model in the east has, however, been constrained by deindustrialisation and high unemployment. What is more, the economic development of the new *Länder* in unified Germany was slower than anticipated and the 'flourishing landscapes' promised by Helmut Kohl failed to emerge. As the economy recovers, institutions of social partnership are not automatically emerging and it is harder for trade unions to establish these institutions in new firms, many of which are SMEs. Table 4.1 shows the different coverage of works councils in east and west.

The success of the German model in eastern Germany was also constrained by tenacious informal institutions of the ex-GDR, that is, the different culture that survived the collapse of the old regime. The informal constraints are both the residual cultures and norms of the GDR and the cultures acquired in the process of transition and adaptation. Informal constraints particularly affected trade unions and gradually, disappointment and disillusionment translated into membership loss. Basing their assessment on their past experience of the FDGB unions, east Germans overestimated the degree of influence that west German trade unions have to shape industrial and national politics. The expectation in the east, that the unions of the west would be able to secure jobs and high incomes was not realised. Also, west German unions appeared to be less evident in everyday life than those of the FDGB, which had a visible union presence in every firm. Employees detached themselves from the DGB and its unions as they could not see how it positively differentiated from the

Table 4.1 Incidence and coverage of works councils in Germany

Size interval (no. employees)	West			East			Unified		
	Incidence[a]	Coverage[b]	Share[c]	Incidence[a]	Coverage[b]	Share[c]	Incidence[a]	Coverage[b]	Share[c]
5–20	9.3	10.5	25.7	7.8	9.8	27.8	9.1	10.4	26.0
21–50	29.9	31.5	14.8	29.9	30.8	18.4	29.9	31.3	15.4
51–100	52.9	53.4	11.4	51.2	51.3	13.1	52.6	53.0	11.7
101–200	68.3	69.5	11.5	69.1	69.7	11.7	68.7	69.5	11.6
201–500	81.4	82.6	14.1	76.2	77.4	12.8	80.6	81.8	13.9
500+	93.3	93.5	22.5	82.1	86.3	16.2	91.7	92.6	21.4
Average	16.6	54.1		15.4	47.1		16.3	53.0	

Notes: [a] denotes the proportion of establishments in the class interval having works councils; [b] denotes the proportion of employees in the class interval employed in firms with works councils; [c] denotes the employment share of the class interval. All data are weighted.

Source: IAB Establishment Panel 2000, cited in J. T Addison, L. Bellmann, C. Schnabel and J. Wagner (2002) *The Long Awaited Reform of the German Works Constitution Act*, IZA Discussion Paper 422, Bonn: IZA: 39.

FDGB. If anything, it appeared to have less power. There was also resent-
ment of the interference of west German personnel. Hyman (1996: 7)
notes that installing the long-established institutional arrangements of
the west over to the east was carried out by a western professional elite
which was accountable to the central authorities of the west. The outcome
of this was 'asymmetrical representation' involving 'the predominance of
external actors and their neglect of or insecurity to "local" views or preferences' (Wiesenthal 1994: 11, cited in Hyman 1996). In short, members
and potential members were reluctant or unable to identify with what was
regarded as an import from the west. Furthermore, as the situation in the
job market worsened, loyalties tended to fall on the side of the employer
who hired and fired and not the union, which was perceived to irritate the
situation with unrealistic demands.

From a west German point of view, the imperfect operationalisation of
west German trade union organisations is blamed on the cultural legacy
of the GDR. The east Germans were criticised for lacking a culture of
opposition (*Widerstandskultur*) and culture of solidarity (*Solidatitätskul-
tur*) (Schmidt 1995). East German members perceived the role of unions
as being representatives on their behalf and were at first reluctant to get
personally involved with campaigning and organisation. In the main,
they still saw themselves as consumers of services provided by unions as
was the case with the FDGB. By contrast the organisation of the DGB and
its unions rely greatly on voluntary efforts, close identification with the
unions and its work as well as active campaigning.

Informal constraints also affected institutions of collective bargaining.
Hyman (1996: 7) notes that the realm of wage bargaining 'followed priorities which were determined in the west and shaped by western interests –
or at least by a pan-German view of interest representation in which the
numerical predominance of the old [FRG] inevitably proved decisive'. The
flexibility introduced into east German wage bargaining did not corre-
spond with west German priorities. However, it appears that east Germans
are willing to accept these not as an ideal but as an alternative preferable to
unemployment. This flexibility is continuously overlooked in discussions
about wage bargaining since unification, and trade unions still demand
wage equalisation.

Legally, the organisations and institutions of the German model were
successfully transferred to the new *Länder*. The transfer has, however, not
been matched by successful operationalisation because the necessary conditions of industrial production and employment which would be
required for this do not prevail. Moreover, the culture and identity of east

German economic actors was formed during socialist industrialism in the GDR and through the experiences of post-*Wende* transition, not during the conditions of capitalist unitary industrialism. The imposition of the unitary, industrial institutional framework of west Germany means that any leapfrogging potential in the east has been restricted. The new *Länder* were able neither to leapfrog, nor to make full use of, the virtuous effects of German model. Since the institutional framework of the German model is not as well institutionalised in the east, there is more potential for it to innovate. There is evidence that in the new *Länder* there is less attachment to this model and that socio-economic actors have a more reflexive attitude and are more willing to innovate with alternative organisational structures. Some – mostly from the east – have argued that the east should be allowed to develop in a more autonomous way (Fichter 1994; Hartung 1997; Kurbjuhn and Fichter 1993; Pohl 1997; Siekmeier 1998). West German resistance to deviations in the east from the German model remains strongly in place. For example, in summer 2003 IG Metall launched a campaign to reduce the average working week in the east to the thirty-five hour standard of the west. This campaign ended in disaster. IG Metall was forced to stop the industrial action without any concessions; this was the first time that this had happened in any German industrial dispute in the post-1945 era.

The limits to technological transformation in the west

The institutions of the German model did not have a virtuous effect on the east German economy. Increasingly, there are indications that the beneficial impact of these institutions may now have reached its limits even in the west (Streeck 1997). Indeed, Grundig, the producer of electrical appliances, and a symbol of post-war German manufacturing excellence, was declared bankrupt in May 2003.

Herrigel (1997) argues that the very institutional configuration that saw German industry through the post-war golden age and the technological transformation of the 1980s has been failing to perform in the same virtuous way since the mid-1990s. He claims that 'these institutionalized features of German industrial life played a very significant role in the post-World War II success of German producers, but now they constitute, at least in their current form, obstacles to effective adjustment to the challenge of alternate forms of flexibility' (Herrigel 1997: 187). The institutional framework could support the transformation of existing production but it is, compared with US and Japanese rivals, too slow, rigid and inflexible for innovating, bringing new products on to the market or integrating new technologies into the production process.

The problem appears to be that firms are too rigidly structured and too hierarchical. Management structures are functionally divided so that each department specialises in a particular function such as purchasing, marketing, developing, finance or production (Herrigel 1997: 190). Firms were designed to promote excellent vertical lines of communication between management and shop-floor workers which allowed for flexibility in production as management and workers could rapidly agree on solutions to production problems. However, the structures which allow for vertical communication work against effective cross-departmental or cross-functional communication and co-operation (191). There is, Herrigel argues, not enough horizontal co-operation within the firm for it to be able to innovate rapidly. As Herrigel puts it 'these clusters of roles and institutions within the German industrial system are proving to be a liability under the current conditions of extremely short product cycles and rapid technological change' (191). Furthermore, the rigidity of the industrial institutional framework has been held responsible for the failure of the so-called new economy to take off in Germany. The knowledge economy at first tended to be housed in the industrial sector and regulated by the industrial order and rather than being established in new firms with new organisation and management structures.

Yet it has proven extremely difficult to implement the necessary institutional changes to put German industrial production in line with its major competitors. Herrigel argues that:

> few producers, large or small, have been able to overcome the opposition of entrenched groupings of skilled workers who, when threatened with the loss of status through incorporation into teams that deny the boundaries of former jurisdictional specializations or independent departments, have resisted the redefinition and dilution of their functional areas of power. (193)

Indeed while institutions of social partnership are able to assist in the general transformation of production, they tend to act as a barrier to any systemic change that threatens their own position.

There are some recent examples of radical and innovative restructuring of industrial production in German firms. At the end of 1999 the personnel management of the car manufacturer Volkswagen (VW) presented a plan for a pilot project to manufacture cars according to a completely new production model. The plan, referred to as '5000 × 5000', aimed to take on 5,000 new, unemployed workers who would be paid at a fixed monthly rate of 5,000DM (about 2,500 euros) and would produce two new vehicles: a new multi-purpose van and a camper van. The innovations of this scheme are as follows. The new workers would operate in shifts and as teams. In contrast to other workers in VW these team workers have no fixed hours. Instead they are set a target of producing a specific number of vans of a specific quality; if this is met within the normal thirty-five hours per week, then they can stop working, if not then they are required to keep working for as long as is necessary to meet the production target. The better organised the team is, the lower is its working time. There are no provisions for extra payments for overtime, shift work or work on Saturdays. The '5000 × 5000' scheme represents a radical departure from traditional production methods. It seeks to introduce flexibly, non-hierarchical production methods into a traditional sector of manufacturing and it introduces an alternative configuration of traditional industrial institutions of social partnership. The details of '5000 × 5000' were agreed with the metalworkers union, IG Metall, though it has been argued that the union had little choice but to accept this scheme as VW was otherwise threatening to shift production to Portugal or Slovakia (Scheele 2000).

Reform of works councils

This chapter has raised some concerns about the relevance and suitability of the industrial institutions of the German model in the contemporary, postindustrial age. On the one hand, they seem to have paved the way for successful technological transformation in the 1980s. On the other hand, in their current form they appear to hinder more the more radical transformations that are necessary both in the old and new *Länder*. This final section looks at recent reforms to works councils legislation to assess whether updating these laws improves the potential of the German model to support manufacturing today.

Concerns about the falling coverage of works councils in the German economy and the relevance of institutions of codetermination for the German model were raised in the mid-1990s at the height of the *Standortdebatte*. It was recognised that while these institutions are well embedded in the traditional areas of the German economy (in large, autarkic firms), there are growing areas of economic activity which are codetermination-free zones or blank spots. A survey of works council coverage from 2000 found that works councils exist in only 16.3 per cent of all German establishments. However, these firms with works councils cover 53 per cent of the workforce (Addision *et al.* 2002: 13). The blank spots in works council coverage are mostly in SMEs and in the new and growing service sector (Addison *et al.* 2002: 8). Works councils are least likely to exist where teamworking practices are common (this is usually in SMEs) and where use is made of the newest production technology (Addison *et al.* 2002: 15). Works council coverage is also lower in the new *Länder*, and in larger firms there in particular.

In 1996 a specialist commission on codetermination was set up to discuss these institutions of social partnership and their relevance for the German model in the present era. The commission was made up of high-ranking scientists, economists, unionists and politicians. The commission reported in 1998 that codetermination remains an important and valuable institutions for the German *Standort* but that it needed to be reformed. It made no concrete proposals for reform, but raised concerns about the growing blank spots in codetermination. The DGB made more concrete recommendations for reform. They demanded more works councils, more works councillors, more paid full-time works councillors and more codetermination rights for works councils (DGB 1998). On election in September 1998, the SPD-Green coalition pledged to reform the laws on works councils and the new law – the Works Constitution Reform Act – was passed in the Bundestag on 22 June 2001 and in the Bundesrat on 13 July 2001. It became effective on 28 July 2001. The new law makes it easier to establish works councils in smaller firms. Employees are permitted to elect more works councillors on a paid, full-time basis and works councils have new rights and areas of codetermination.

Works councils will in future be larger. Table 4.2 shows that the threshold for the membership of works councils has fallen, so smaller firms will in future have more works councillors. The structure of works councils has become more diverse. In enterprises with more than one establishment, works councils can be formed across some or all of the constituent establishments. The creation of works councils in SMEs employing between five and fifty employees is facilitated through a simplified voting procedure. This procedure can also be extended to establishments with fifty-one to a hundred employees.

Under the new law, employers are required to make full provision for a full-time works councillor in establishments with 200 or more employees instead of 300 as before. The threshold for additional full-time works councillors has also been lowered. The employer has to furnish the works

Table 4.2   Membership of the works council by establishment size: former and new legislation

Old 1972		New 2001	
No. of employees	No. of works councillors	No. of employees	No. of works councillors
5–20	1	5–20	1
21–50	3	21–50	3
51–150	5	51–100	5
151–300	7	101–200	7
301–600	9	201–400	9
601–1000	11	401–700	11
1001–2000	15	701–1000	13
2001–3000	19	1001–1500	15
3001–4000	23	1501–2000	17
4001–5000	27	2001–2500	19
5001–7000	29	2501–3000	21
7001–9000	31	3001–3500	23
		3501–4000	25
		4001–4500	27
		4501–5000	29
		5001–6000	31
		6001–7000	33
		7001–9000	35
9000+	The no. of works councillors is increased by 2 members for each incremental 3000 employees	9000+	Unchanged

Source: J. T Addison, L. Bellmann, C. Schnabel and J. Wagner (2002) *The Long Awaited Reform of the German Works Constitution Act*, IZA Discussion Paper 422, Bonn: IZA.

council office at his own expense with modern information and communication technology. The influence of any single employee in the codetermination process is strengthened by his or her ability to require the works council to debate a particular issue when supported by at least 5 per cent of the workforce. Temporary workers may participate in works council elections if they have been employed for more than three months in the establishment. Youth and trainee representation is increased. In establishments with more than 100 employees representing, say, young workers they would have the right to form their own committees.

Table 4.3   Number of works council members released from their
work duties by establishment size: former and new legislation

Old		New	
No. of employees	No. of paid, full-time works councillors	No. of employees	No. of paid, full-time works councillors
300–600	1	200–500	1
601–1000	2	501 900	2
1001–2000	3	901–1500	3
2001–3000	4	1501–2000	4
3001–4000	5	2001–3000	5
4001–5000	6	3001–4000	6
5001–6000	7	4001–5000	7
6001–7000	8	5001–6000	8
7001–8000	9	6001–7000	9
8001–9000	10	7001–8000	10
9001–10000	11	8001–9000	11
		9000–10000	12
10000+	One further member of the works council for each incremental 2000 employees	10000+	Unchanged

Source: J. T Addison, L. Bellmann, C. Schnabel and J. Wagner (2002) *The Long Awaited Reform of the German Works Constitution Act*, IZA Discussion Paper 422, Bonn: IZA

The new works councils have new rights and there are more areas in which they can voice their opinion. The influence of the works council in matters of employment protection and the training of the workforce is strengthened. This includes the possibility of enforcing training measures that benefit employees whose qualifications are obsolete. Also the works council has codetermination rights in the execution of teamwork. Codetermination on environmental protection issues is explicitly recognised as a function of the works council. Gender equality is facilitated by the requirement that the minority gender at the establishment be represented on the works council at least in proportion to its employment share. Furthermore, the works councils has the right to suggest plans for the promotion of women and make these the subject of human resource planning wherein the employer has to consult the works council. The works council is equipped with formal means to avoid racism and xenophobia in the workplace.

The new law clearly strengthens rather than undermines this institution of social partnership for the postindustrial age. It makes it easier to form works councils in firms in blank spots and it gives works councils more weight and more influence. More powerful works councils will help employees become co-managers in the firm. The idea is that if they have more works councillors, they will be able to develop their own business concepts instead of just reacting to the plans put forward by the management (Viering 2001). Clearly, the institutions of the German model are being reformed and adapted to suit the postindustrial era, rather than being eradicated. The question remains whether the opportunity this new law offers employees to form works councils will be taken up and whether this law will help eradicate blank spots on the codetermination landscape. Also, 98 per cent of firms have fewer than 100 employees and the number of works councillors will remain unchanged in these firms (Viering 2001).

Conclusion: regional patterns of technological transformation

The institutions of the German model have shaped Germany's postindustrial development to an industrial production model. However, as this chapter has shown, unified Germany's development has not entirely followed this trajectory. The decentralised south-west has been even more successful in transforming its industry and maintaining industrial employment than the autarkic north-west. The transfer of the industrial institutions of the German model to the eastern parts of Germany did not lead to a similar technological transformation for three reasons: the east German industrial base was rapidly destroyed after unification; the institutions did not become sufficiently embedded in the east; and the formal institutions of the German model were filled in by informal tenacious institutions of the GDR. The transformation of industry in the east has, as a consequence, been much weaker and extremely varied.

Recent research suggests that the virtuous impact of the German model is no longer leading to technological transformation in the west. It has been suggested that the institutions are too rigid and too slow to adapt to the needs of rapidly changing markets in the global economy. Reform of works councils legislation in 2001 marks a determined effort to adapt these institutions in the current era. However, there is not yet enough evidence to assess the impact of this reform on the German model and its potential to facilitate successful technological transformation in industrial firms.

5

Germany as a knowledge economy

In the knowledge economy variant of the postindustrial economy and society, knowledge is considered the most important commodity and factor of production (Hodgson 1999). Theorists of the knowledge economy argue that it is increasingly knowledge and not technological developments that drives economic growth and innovation. Economies need to concentrate on the production and reproduction of knowledge in order to maintain their position in the international economy. The way to do this is by investing in the production (education and training) and maintenance (health) of human resources. A highly skilled labour force will facilitate the implementation of technological innovations in industrial production and promote the development of professional services in areas such as research, education, business consultancy, advertising and law. Knowledge is considered important because it presents an alternative to the development of a low-skill, low-wage economy. If states can follow the 'high road' to a knowledge economy, then it may be possible to avoid the 'low road' to a deregulated, low-wage service economy (Sabel 1995).

This chapter considers the role of knowledge in the German model. It argues that the German economy and society have always valued highly knowledge, education and training. This fact is reflected in the institutions that developed and became deeply embedded in the industrial era. Knowledge institutions promote the skills and knowledge development of the labour force at all levels from secondary education through to vocational training or higher education. This is further supported by innovation systems which promote strong, incremental innovation (Harding and Soskice 2000; Soskice 1999). Through such institutions Germany has developed as a high-skill and high-wage economy and has undergone successful technological transformation of industrial production to prevent Germany from becoming a low-skill and low-wage service economy.

Germany traditionally has a good reputation as a knowledge and learning economy (Wagner 1998) and it would be easy to conclude that Germany therefore has a competitive advantage in the postindustrial knowledge economy.

However, recently there have been increased concerns about whether the institutions of the German model are producing and reproducing the right kinds of knowledge for the contemporary era, and whether they are able to adapt fast enough. It is becoming apparent that the institutionalised systems of learning and knowledge promote and reproduce traditional kinds of specialist technical knowledge appropriate to the industrial era, but that they are weak at producing new kinds of general knowledge and transferable skills that are required in the new postindustrial paradigm. A number of studies have identified crises in the institutions of knowledge at all levels. For example, the recent OECD PISA evaluation of education systems ranked Germany below the international average. There are also ongoing discussions in Germany about reform of the higher education system to get rid of non-innovative personnel and to prevent a further academic brain drain. This chapter considers Germany's strengths and weaknesses as a knowledge economy and assesses whether the crisis debates concerning schools, vocational training and higher education justify the pessimistic conclusion that Germany is lagging behind in the knowledge economy. It also analyses significant regional differences within Germany and reviews some recent policy developments such as the controversial green card scheme which was introduced in 2001 to address the shortage of specialist IT workers in Germany.

Institutions of knowledge and learning in Germany

Germany is a political economy with a proud tradition of promoting education and training and the production and reproduction of knowledge through stable and embedded institutions (Lepenies 2003). Some of these institutions have a long tradition in Germany; others became institutionalised in the post-1945 period. There are two competing ideals of education in Germany: general and academic; or technical and vocational. On the one hand, education is promoted for its own sake as the general cultural phenomenon of *Bildung* in institutions such as grammar schools and universities. On the other hand, specialist, technical training is promoted in institutions of vocational training such as intermediate school, apprenticeship schemes and through institutions of research and

development to serve the aims of high productivity in industrial production. The German school system is traditionally divided to develop either
academic or vocational knowledge. All children start school when they
are six years old and normally attend primary school (*Grundschule*) for
four years. The education system then sorts pupils according to their level
of academic achievement or preferences into the *Hauptschule, Realschule,
Gymnasium,* or *Gesamtschule.* The *Gymnasium* (grammar school) provides academic education for students who want to go on to study at a
university or a university of applied science (*Fachhochschule*) where they
will study for a postgraduate degree. In a *Gymnasium* considerable
emphasis is put on academic learning, a large variety of subjects are
taught and students are expected to be fairly self-motivated. *Gymnasium*
students attend school for nine years before doing a final university
entrance examination or *Abitur.* After the first six years the students can
specialise in certain areas such as humanities, languages or science. In
comparison to the *Gymnasium,* the *Realschule* (intermediate school)
offers a more vocationally oriented education. The education offered here
is quite broad and subjects are studied in greater depth than at the lower
Hauptschule (main school) which is geared towards students who want to
do an apprenticeship when they have finished school. At the *Hauptschule*
the main emphasis is on teaching practical skills and the application of
theoretical knowledge. In 1969 the *Gesamtschule* (comprehensive school)
was introduced; this combines all three streams in a single institution. But
the coverage of these schools is not uniform across Germany as *Länder*
have their own Ministry for Education and can exercise a certain freedom
in regard to the school system. *Länder* in more conservative areas such as
Bayern or Baden-Württemberg have been less enthusiastic about introducing the *Gesamtschule* than in traditionally social democratic states
such as Nordrhein Westfalen.

School leavers who do not go on to university traditionally enter into
a vocational training system. This offers three-year dual training, that is,
both a theoretical basis taught in a vocational school and practical experience in firms which sponsor the apprentice. This has a long tradition in
Germany and remains a valued institution which has helped maintain
and sustain Germany's high-wage, high-skill economy. According to
Wagner (1998: 2), approximately 70 per cent of young people benefit
from German dual vocational training. This institution also reinforces
the co-ordinated and consensual nature of the German model, as the
traineeships are designed and sustained by social partners and firms participate on a voluntary basis. It produces a high output of skilled and

well-educated employees who provide a basis for Germany's export success and innovation (Wagner 1998). The apprentice system benefits firms in a number of ways. It means that apprentices can be trained to carry out the specific tasks required by the sponsoring firm and so there is no need to retrain new employees (Herrigel 1997). Also, investment in trainees on the part of employers has encouraged long-term and stable employment relationships as employers are reluctant to let their trainees be poached by competitor firms.

Investing in the skills of trainees and workers leads to an incremental innovation system. As Hall and Soskice (2001: 39) explain, the institutional configuration of the German model is able to support incremental innovation because 'the workforce . . . is skilled enough to contribute to such innovations, secure enough to risk suggesting changes to products or process that might alter their job situation, and endowed with enough work autonomy to see these kinds of improvements as a dimension of their job'. The strength of the German economy has come from incremental innovations in the production of capital goods such as machine tools and factory equipment, consumer durables, engines and specialised transport equipment. The incremental innovation system is further supported by the close links that have developed between industry and universities and other research institutes such as the Max Planck Institutes, Higher Education Institutes or the Fraunhofer Society (Harding and Soskice 2000).

The innovation system has been criticised for being top heavy and for failing to innovate in new areas such as biotechnology or IT. However, Harding and Soskice (2000) are optimistic that the German innovation system will be able to adapt. They argue (90) that 'the German economy has historically proven itself resilient to major shifts in techno-economic paradigms and there is no reason to suggest that the latest phase of IT or biotechnology should be any different'. They conclude:

> the German system generally and technology policy in particular appears remarkably suitable for sustaining the country's traditional strengths in producing hi-tech and high added-value incremental innovations and adapting itself, albeit relatively slowly to exogenous paradigm shifts. The inherent dynamism of the system is such that it can successfully incorporate both markets and new innovations. (99)

The crisis of institutions of knowledge

While Harding and Soskice draw a positive conclusion about the future of the incremental innovation system in Germany, other studies have in recent years identified serious problems in other institutions of knowledge and learning (*Spiegel* 2002). The identified crises spanned schools, the vocational system and universities. To address the shortfalls, a series of reform measures have been proposed and implemented.

The German education system has received a bad press ever since 2001 when the OECD published its PISA report. This study compared the quality of education in thirty-two industrial nations. German schoolchildren performed below average on all the main indicators, with the following rankings in the main subjects: twenty-first out of thirty-one in reading; twentieth out of thirty-one in mathematics and twentieth out of thirty-one in natural science. These results appear to undermine Germany's reputation as a learning and learned nation (Lepenies 2003) and calls into question its status as a state which will perform well in a knowledge and learning economy. As Darnstädt *et al.* (2001: 68) put it, 'in Deutschland herrschen ausweislich der Pisa-Studie Verhältnisse, die eines Hightech-Staates nicht würdig sind' (the PISA study demonstrates that Germany's education conditions do not earn it the label of a high-tech economy).

How can Germany's poor performance be explained? Hodgson (1999: 75) claims that in the new economy the capacity to learn is an essential skill. Learning he defines as 'a process of problem-formation and problem-solving'. Germany's weakness in the PISA study was precisely that it was weak at problem-based learning. The German school system concentrates on input and processing; absorbing canons of information and then engaging in 'bestreiten, zerreden, beschönen' (discussing and debating a lot but without really reaching any conclusions) (Darnstädt *et al.* 2001: 50). Students have less experience in problem-solving or in producing outputs which can be assessed against learning objectives.

The weakness of the German schoolchildren in reading literacy suggested that pupils were weak at extracting information, interpreting this information and then relating it to a real-life situation. While 10 per cent of German schoolchildren were unable to extract any basic information from a text, a further 13 per cent were unable to evaluate the information or relate it to an everyday context. In no other country was the gap between the best and the worst readers larger than in Germany. The worst performers were non-German native speakers and children from socially disadvantaged families. Chancellor Schröder (2003) commented that:

in no comparable industrial country does social background play such a large part in educational opportunity as in Germany . . . We must change the situation whereby . . . the chances of attending a grammar school for a young person from the upper classes is six to ten times greater than for a young person from a working class family. It is a scandal that one in four foreign pupils leaves school without a qualification.

Germany's weak performance in PISA has been attributed to the fact that, at six or seven years old, a child's schooling starts too late; by this time basic language skills will have been acquired. This disadvantages children from lower social classes and non-native speaking families as they are less likely to attend a kindergarten and, in the case of the latter group, often have only spoken their native tongue at home. Also, it has been suggested that German children spend too little time at school; the school day runs from 0800 to lunchtime. German pupils spend less time in the classroom than in other countries and they have less time to apply their knowledge and more time to undertake non-learning activities. The German school system has also been criticised for dividing children into educational streams too quickly and for directing disproportionate amounts of education spending at the best pupils in grammar schools. Increasing numbers of students have been going to *Gymnasien* because of falling standards in *Realschulen* and *Hauptschulen*, and because of ambitions to go on to university rather than vocational training. This has further reduced standards in the vocational schools. The *Hauptschule* is now considered a school for non-German native speakers, children from socially disadvantaged families and students with learning difficulties. These less academic schools are too underfunded to offer a decent standard of education.

In response to the PISA study, the German Federal Minister for Education and Research highlighted five key action points: education in Germany needs to begin earlier and kindergarten provision needs to be expanded; more money needs to be invested in primary schools; there needs to be more individual support for children; full-day schooling needs to be introduced in Germany so that school pupils can actively acquire and apply knowledge and skills; there needs to be a more practical orientation in teacher training; and schools in Germany need more autonomy (Bulmahm 2002). In 2002 the SPD–Green coalition agreement set out plans to implement some of the necessary reforms and these plans were taken forward in Schröder's Agenda 2010 plan in spring 2003. The government has proposed to expand childcare for the under-threes so that every fifth child would have access to a kindergarten place. This would mean that children of all social classes from German and non-German speaking families would have access to pre-school education and this would place all six-year-old school starters on a more equal footing. The government has also proposed to invest a total of 4 billion euros in the development and expansion of all-day schooling between 2003 and 2005. This would give students an opportunity to spend more time applying their knowledge, it would allow for more individual supervision of pupils and should help eradicate some of the worst inequalities between social groups. As well as introducing all-day schools, the government intends to draw up national education standards, against which performance can be measured, and to invest in the continuing training and professional development of teachers so that they are able to promote better standards and individual treatment of students.

The new economic paradigm has also challenged the viability and sustainability of a vocational training system. It is unclear whether firms will be willing to invest in skilling their labour force in a globalised economy in which production can be easily transferred to any other part of the world. According to Wagner (1998), the problems of the German vocational system are threefold. The costs of training apprentices has risen for the sponsoring firms because the shift in focus towards the theoretical part of the dual training system meaning that trainees spend less time on productive work in the firm. This is coupled with the recession in the 1990s which made an increasing number of firms withdraw from the system as they were not prepared to invest in training.

It is also unclear whether the German vocational training system is able to adapt quickly enough to incorporate new production methods and newly emerging skills and professions. In other words, the German vocational system may not be able to reproduce the appropriate skills and knowledge for the postindustrial knowledge economy. On a general level, the German training system has been updated to include training in new skills such as social competencies and teamworking. However, the number of occupations offered by the dual system reduced from 901 in 1950 to 375 in 1995 (Wagner 1998: 10). This consolidation includes the new occupations that have been added to the system. In the mid-1990s the demand for new areas of training was addressed and five new traineeships in occupations associated with multimedia were designed. Other areas have been identified in information technology, safety, leasing, environment and fast food. In 1995, training schemes in twenty-six new occupations were introduced and fifty others were modernised (Wagner 1998: 22). But, as Wagner points out (22), updating existing skills profiles and developing new areas of training are slow because the German system is based on co-operation and consent by employers, trade unions and the government.

Recent debates in Germany have identified a severe crisis in the German higher education system, and an urgent need to reform its institutions. Germany is renowned for the comparatively long time it takes students to complete a university degree. Students graduate at the average age of twenty-six. There are also concerns about the high numbers of students at German universities, many of whom do not complete their studies. As Hielscher *et al.* (2002: 56) point out German universities are overflowing and underfinanced. Universities in Germany have sought to provide a uniform provision of all academic subjects. This means there is little specialisation, and no real international centres of excellence. In addition it is notoriously difficult to reform Germany universities. They are over-regulated and protected by entrenched interests of lobbies, such as professors. Since universities are *Länder* institutions, solutions will vary across Germany. Proposed solutions to the crisis of German universities have included charging fees for students who go beyond the standard recommended study time, charging fees for all students, halting the intake of new students in Berlin universities until a significant number of long-term students left the system and introducing a bachelor degree qualification instead of expecting all students to complete a postgraduate qualification (*Hauptstudium*).

Crisis accounts of the German university system have also highlighted the brain drain of academic personnel at junior and professorial levels to foreign universities or to business because there are no German universities with international reputations or because the bureaucracy of German universities stifles innovation (BMBF 2002: 9). The concern is that the conditions at German universities do not support and lock in the most innovative and productive academics, and that instead too much dead wood remains in the system. Indeed a significant number of German Nobel prize winners now live and work in the USA (*Spiegel* 2002).

A particular concern is how conditions can be improved for junior academics to prevent a brain drain at this level. Many junior academics leave the academy because of the long time it takes to qualify and poor job opportunities and poor conditions of employment that exist for junior staff. Following the PhD, which is rarely completed before the age of thirty, junior academics are traditionally required to embark on a second thesis, the *Habilitation*, before they can apply for permanent professorial posts. The hurdle of the *Habilitation* means that academics are usually over forty by the time they can apply for a permanent job at professorial level, and this particularly disadvantages female academics. Junior academics also have to rely on temporary contracts and insecure working conditions until they make it to professor. Contracts have been kept below five years so academics do not have the right to claim a permanent contract. Limited (and declining) numbers of permanent contracts are only available at professorial level following the successful completion of the *Habilitation*. An academic with the *Habilitation* qualification (a *Habil*) is not allowed to apply for a permanent professorship at the same institutions that awarded the *Habilitation*. As professors, academics in Germany enjoy an exceptionally high degree of independence and security. However, until they have reached that stage, German academics are required to endure long periods of dependence on professorial supervisors before they are allowed teach and research independently. This stifles innovation, motivation and creativity.

A number of reforms in German universities have been passed recently to seek to retain innovative academics by introducing performance-related pay and improving working conditions for junior staff. At the same time, strict limits to the length of time junior academics can spend on temporary contracts have been introduced in an attempt to rid the system of ineffective academics. In 1998 higher education law was reformed to make the funding of universities and professorial pay more performance related, to introduce more evaluation in teaching and research and the accreditation of degree programmes, and to introduce bachelor and masters programmes. A second wave of reforms, passed in 2001, aims to make young academics more independent, to promote their creativity and motivation, and to try to improve Germany's international position in research and education.

In order to improve the independence and working conditions of junior academics, the new framework law introduced a new academic position for postdoctorates – the junior professor. These academics are given more freedom to pursue their own research and teaching agenda. Instead of working for an individual chair or professor, they work independently within a university department. They have their own budget, can apply independently for funding, and can supervise PhD students. Junior professors are no longer expected to complete a *Habilitation* in order to qualify for a full professorship. Instead they are assessed after three and then six years by a faculty committee. The *Habilitation* will exist in parallel to the junior professors until 2008. To get rid of ineffective academics the law removes the five-year time limit on temporary contracts.

In its place it introduces a longer time limit of twelve years from finishing a first degree to professorship. This means that if after twelve years on temporary contracts (six before and six after the PhD, and including any time spent abroad) junior academics have not managed to obtain a professorship, no further temporary contacts can be issued to them.

These reforms have been widely criticised and it is not at all clear whether they will achieve their stated aims of improving the quality of university teaching and research, supporting innovation and making university careers more open and predictable. Bahle (2002: 11) argues that these reforms are unlikely to succeed because they have been implemented in a top-down 'patriarchal manner' without really understanding the situation in German universities and despite opposition from many specialists in university education. Bahle (2002: 9–11) identifies five key problems with the new system. The first is that junior professors will be expected to take on a heavier teaching load than those following the *Habilitation* route, as well as fulfilling the same research requirements. The second problem is that junior professors might in fact be less, rather than more, independent. The new internal evaluation that junior professors are to go through 'opens up immense possibilities for influence and exploitation'. Bahle argues that 'the old feudal regime of chairs and chair assistants' is potentially being replaced with 'new regime of collective exploitation' which is unlikely to improve the situation of young academics. It is hard to see that junior professors will be able to work independently in a system that traditionally relies on hierarchies and dependencies. Thirdly, with the introduction of the junior professor the old system of obligatory mobility after *Habilitation* has been removed. Bahle argues that 'influence and exploitation are all the more likely, as the new law explicitly provides for, indeed invites, departments to make use of internal tenure tracks'. Not only will junior professors be able to apply for tenure at the same university, retiring professors will be able to select the candidate they would like to succeed them. According to Bahle, 'this opens up immense scope for conspiracy and departmental politics, the victims of which will be the junior professors and their independence'. He goes on, 'there is also a real danger that universities will become still more like closed shops, producing and reproducing the same ideas, themes and methods' and that the reforms will do nothing to promote genuine innovation. Fourthly, the assessment procedure for junior professors is more arbitrary now that the *Habilitation* has been removed. Although the second qualification was considered a torturous task, it was a relatively uncomplicated minimum requirement for comparing candidates on the open market. Bahle argues, 'with the abolition of the *Habilitation* and the possibility of internal tenure-tracks, all calculable qualification criteria have gone'. There is a lack of transparency in the new system which will affect the young researchers and the quality of German universities. Finally, in the interim period, when junior professorships and the *Habilitation* run concurrently, there will be unfair and unequal competition for professorial posts between holders of a *Habilitation* and the new junior professors. *Habils* will have more experience, and will be more highly respected by existing professors within the system; junior professors will be on the whole younger and will have more teaching experience.

In sum it appears that insecure conditions will continue for junior academics. What is more, the number of permanent professorial posts is currently being reduced as the professors from the 1960s expansion of higher education go into retirement. There is not enough funding for them to be replaced and few junior academics will have a reasonable expectation of getting a full professorship on successful completion of the junior professorship. This will not necessarily encourage PhD students to stay in academia, and it will not keep junior professors in Germany. Most significantly, the growing insecurity of the labour market in universities has serious implications for the institutions that promote Germany's traditional model of incremental innovation, which relies on stable, long-term strategies.

Knowledge and learning in the new *Länder*

The institutions of knowledge and learning in Germany are in crisis and need to be reformed. However any adjustment to the existing institutions appears to be hard to implement because of the entrenched interests that defend the status quo. This problem appears to be less significant in the new *Länder*. At the time of the *Wende*, the west German knowledge institutions were transferred wholesale to the east and the east Germans were obliged to adapt to the new circumstances. This experience has the potential to give the new *Länder* an advantage over the old *Länder* in the transition to the knowledge economy. Hodgson (1999: 74) points out that 'especially in a rapidly developing socio-economic system, individuals face changing institutions, rules and technologies. We are obliged to adapt to the evolving reality: we are required to learn'. Since Germans in the east were forced to adapt rapidly to a new political and socio-economic situation, they may have a greater willingness and capacity for learning.

What is more, there is evidence that the institutions of knowledge which were transferred to the east at the time of unification are less well embedded than in the west. Since there is less cultural attachment to the institutions, this potentially facilitates a faster reform process. Indeed, universities in the new *Länder* are more open to innovation. As a Hielscher *et al.* (2002: 58) put it '[es] herrscht an vielen Unis in der ehemaligen DDR eine Aufbruchsstimmung. Die alten Strukturen waren zerbrochen, und die Offenheit für Neues ist noch immer größer als im Westen, der akademische Betrieb zudem von überschaubarer Größe' (east German universities are ready for a new start; they are more likely to experiment and try out new things). Also, a study carried out by the Centrum für Hochschulentwicklung (Centre for the Development of Higher Education or CHE) compared the performance of universities in the sixteen different *Länder*. The universities were judged on the following criteria: how students rate the performance of the university departments, how research active the universities are, how long it takes on average to complete a degree and what reputation the university departments have. The CHE study ranked the universities in Thüringen, Mecklenburg-Vorpommern, Bayern, Sachsen und Baden-Württemberg at the top of the league. Significantly, three of these five top universities are in the new *Länder*. In fact the east German universities came top overall because of the high quality of the student experience there. The universities in the east are not mass universities, there is a good staff–student ratio and supervision of student projects. Also, the average duration of studies in the east is lower than in the west (Finetti 2002: 5).

The potential for the east to leapfrog the west as a knowledge economy is also apparent in that a number of reforms planned to modernise Germany's institutions of knowledge and learning mark a return to the institutions which existed in the GDR. Although East Germany was not exactly the most successful knowledge economy, the *Wende* clearly eradicated key GDR institutions which supported the growth of a knowledge economy. For example, the key policy recommendations that came out of Germany's poor performance in the PISA study was to introduce a better provision of pre-school care and to introduce all-day schooling. In the GDR, both these institutions existed for all infants and schoolchildren. Ironically, Finland, one of the nations ranked top in the PISA study, attributed its success in the PISA ranking to the fact that it copied the GDR school system (Lepenies 2003: 61).

The eastern part of Germany could turn to its advantage the fact that institutions of knowledge are less embedded and that, following unification, it was forced to learn, adapt and innovate. It could create innovative training schemes which promote the knowledge and skills that the western part of Germany is lacking. Some attempts have been made to develop the south-east of Germany as an area of specialism in the field of high-technology IT – an east German 'Silicon Valley' (Bowley 1998). However, it has not been successful at producing the right skills to create a high-technology niche.

The potential of the new *Länder* to leapfrog the west as a knowledge economy has been restricted by the fact that there has been a chronic lack of investment in human capital in the east. Policy in the post-unification period concentrated on capital investment and cash transfer payments to the new *Länder*, which then flowed back to the west German economy as the cash was used to buy west German goods. Innovation, research and development and training are significantly weaker in the east than in the west and there are no research institutes which specifically promote strategies that will benefit the east German economy (Thierse 2001). Also, although the institutions of vocational training were transferred whole-sale to the to the east at the time of unification, the collapse of the east German economy meant that there are not enough training places being offered. The supply has been growing slowly, in crafts and services more than in industry, but there is still not enough to meet demand. Young east Germans increasingly are migrating to the west or abroad to take up a training post or employment. In 2000, the number of eighteen to thirty year olds migrating from the new *Länder* was around 33,400 (Repke *et al.* 2002) and this brain drain will severely affect the development of the east German knowledge economy.

Employment in the knowledge economy

Germany's priority has been to follow the high road to a knowledge-based postindustrial economy. However, the growth in knowledge-intensive employment in the professions of the new economy in Germany has been slow. Moreover, there appears to be a clear discrepancy between the skills that are being produced and the demand for those professionals. In recent years, large numbers of highly qualified graduates in the knowledge industries such as telecommunications, consultancy, advertising and law have been made unemployed and the number of new jobs being advertised in these professions is falling (Finke *et al.* 2002). Between July 2001 and July 2002, unemployment in consultancy, advertising and law grew by

56.5 per cent, 47.8 per cent and 29.6 per cent respectively (Finke *et al.* 2002: 28–9). At the same time, however, there is a strong demand for professionals with knowledge skills that the German knowledge institutions do not appear able to create.

Since the late 1990s there has been growing concern in German business that there are not enough skilled IT employees and that, as a consequence, the growth of the new economy in Germany was being restricted. At the end of the 1990s employers claimed that 75,000 qualified people were needed in this area (Welsch 2000: 1473). The demand for IT specialists is growing rapidly, but the apprenticeship system is not managing to keep up with new developments. Also, while more people are registering to study computer-related subjects in German universities, the number who actually complete their studies is falling (Welsch 2000: 1474–5).

In 1998 companies began to demand a green card scheme to recruit 30,000 qualified IT specialists from abroad. The government responded to these demands in two ways. It drew up a strategy for increasing the supply of IT specialists within Germany (Welsch 2000: 1476) and in 2000 it launched a debate about the possibility of issuing green cards to IT specialists from India and eastern Europe. In the German context, a green card is merely a temporary permit for a specific professional group and is not, as in the American scheme, a long-term residency and work permit and the opportunity to apply for citizenship after a five-year period.

The German green card proposals were published in April 2000 and legislation was passed in August 2000. It was anticipated that around 20,000 green cards would be issued for experts in information and communication technology from non-EU states for a period of five years. These IT specialists would only be allowed to enter Germany with evidence of an employment contract, and if they are able to demonstrate that they have the appropriate academic or professional qualifications and an adequate standard of German. These proposals were welcomed by employers but the trade unions' response was less enthusiastic. While unions did not oppose the scheme in principle, they highlighted the fact that there were 31,000 unemployed IT specialists in Germany who could be quickly retrained. They also argued that business should invest in vocational training and in retraining Germans whose skills are slightly out of date rather than complaining to government about the lack of supply of trained IT specialists. Unions also claimed that a large number of German workers with appropriate skills could be found by freeing up computer specialists whose time was wasted by carrying out mundane office work that could easily be carried out by less qualified staff (Wirtschaftswoche 2000).

Despite the vociferous calls from business for a green card scheme, the actual take-up of green cards after the launch of the scheme was very slow. By November 2000 only 2,970 permits had been issued. This slow take-up has been explained in two ways. Some suspect that the IT-industry exaggerated the gap between supply and demand for IT specialists in Germany in order to shirk its duty to invest in training. Alternatively, it has been claimed that taking work in Germany is an unattractive option for IT specialists, who are in high demand in all advanced capitalist states (Martin and Werner 2000). For one thing, German firms introduced strict German language requirements and some even required green card holders to have a German academic or vocational qualification. Green card holders are only offered a limited period of residence rather than the option to apply for permanent citizenship. Many of those who took up jobs in IT on the green card scheme subsequently lost their jobs when the new economy collapsed in 2000 and are under pressure to find a new position to avoid being deported. Finally, IT specialists might be less inclined to take up work in Germany given its ambivalent attitude towards immigration and immigrants, the highly publicised incidents of extreme right-wing violence, and some extremely controversial political campaigns against the green card scheme. In the 2000 *Land* election in Nordrhein Westfalen the CDU opposed the scheme with the outrageous campaigning slogan 'Kinder statt Inder', implying that Germany should be investing in 'children, not Indians' (Welsch 2000: 1479–80).

Conclusion

Germany has always had a priority to promote a high-skill and high-wage economy, and has in the past facilitated this in various institutions of knowledge and learning. Germany favoured a high-road transition to a postindustrial economy which comprised technological transformation and services in high-skilled professions. On the whole, it seems that Germany has the potential to become a successful knowledge economy if it is able to promote problem-based learning and accelerate the speed at which new skills are being produced and reproduced. However, in their current form these institutions do not appear able rapidly to produce and reproduce the right kinds of knowledge to make Germany a strong and competitive knowledge economy. Reforms to address Germany's shortcomings as a knowledge economy are under way, but it is a slow process and in many instances it is not clear the reforms will lead to the desired outcome.

In the new *Länder* knowledge institutions are not as well embedded as in the west and there is evidence of reform and innovation since 1989–90. Also, recent reforms in German are returning the east to a number of the traditional institutions of the GDR with which Germans in the new *Länder* are familiar. However, there has been inadequate investment in human capital and research and development in the east, and this is still too low for eastern Germany to develop a comparative advantage in the knowledge economy. As a priority, the east needs to halt the brain drain of young people caused by their migration to the west and abroad.

6

Postindustrial trajectories in unified Germany

This book has introduced three contrasting paradigms of postindustrial transition – the service sector economy, the model of technological transformation and the knowledge – and has emphasised the fact that states take different routes. There is no single paradigm of postindustrialism to which all political economies are required to converge if they are to remain competitive in the current phase of capitalism. In a similar way to the critics of other convergence theories, such as globalisation and the end of history theory, this book has argued that national political economies will not follow a single path of postindustrial development. There are, in other words, different, coexisting postindustrial trajectories in the global economy.

National models of capitalism exploit their competitive advantage by adapting in different ways to the new economic paradigm. The UK and the USA are, for example, taking the service sector route. A number of dominant accounts of Germany as a postindustrial state have emphasised the fact that its service economy is underdeveloped and have argued that Germany needs to catch up with more advanced service sector economies such as the Anglo-Saxon states to overcome its crises. Generalisations about Germany as underdeveloped in postindustrial economy are, however, misleading and wrong. More useful accounts recognise that, although Germany has not rapidly developed its service sector economy, it has instead successfully adapted its industrial production to new technological developments and retained high levels of employment in industrial production.

A closer analysis of the postindustrial political economy of unified Germany reveals, however, that the technological transformation account of Germany does not apply equally across the whole of the economy. The key finding of this book is that unified Germany's postindustrial economy and society is not a homogenous phenomenon, but highly complex and differentiated. Postindustrial transition is not a uniform or unitary development within unified Germany since there are a number of different industrial and deindustrialised bases which are currently transforming. This analysis of unified Germany reveals a crucial reality of postindustrial economies. Not only are there are coexisting postindustrial trajectories in the global economy; there are also different paths to postindustrial economy and society within national economies.

This chapter concludes *Postindustrial Germany* by highlighting some of the main points made in this book. It summarises the way formal and informal institutions have shaped Germany's postindustrial development. It also outlines how variations in these institutions lead to regional paths of postindustrial development. It then argues that the key to Germany's success as a postindustrial economy is to allow its postindustrial trajectories to coexist. The German model needs to be flexible enough to accommodate, indeed encourage, the development of regional postindustrial niches, so that all regions are able to play to their inherent strengths. From this perspective, the chapter then revisits the issue of the crisis of the German model of capitalism. It argues that this crisis is not the consequence of Germany's failure to converge with more advanced postindustrial states. Rather, it is argued that it is the outcome of persisting with a unitary industrial institutional framework which constrains the potential development of some elements within a diverse German postindustrial economy. The German model needs to be reformed so that it is able to respond rapidly, and in a differentiated manner, to the diverse challenges thrown up by Germany's coexisting postindustrial trajectories.

The impact of institutions on Germany's postindustrial transition

The postindustrial diversity inherent in the global economy and within national political economies can be explained by contrasting patterns of distinctive and embedded patterns of formal and informal institutions. The paths of postindustrialism that states, or regions within states, take are enabled and constrained by the institutional configurations which underpins them. Germany's transition to a postindustrial economy and society can be explained, therefore, by the impact that the institutions of the post-1945 industrial German model had on postindustrial transformation.

The formal institutional framework of the German model developed to support and promote stable high-skill, high-wage male employment in the industrial economy. Institutions of social partnership, training and innovation were well embedded to support this outcome. The welfare state was structured to promote male employment and reduce levels of female employment and the need for private services. This formal institutional framework was accompanied by an informal framework which valued the norms of industrial production and bred a culture of inclusive, consensual incremental decision-making. These combined to promote incremental and stable economic development and prevent radical change that might lead to instability.

This set of formal and informal institutions created favourable conditions for Germany's path of postindustrial transition – technological transformation. It promoted a high-knowledge and high-skill economy which favoured the incremental innovation in existing technologies. Crucially, this facilitated a gradual transformation of industrial production from mass production to flexible specialisation. Also, it has meant that even though rates of employment in manufacturing have fallen gradually in the 1990s, there has not been a collapse of industrial employment in western Germany comparable to 1980s' Britain.

The same institutional framework has also constrained a rapid development of service sector activity, and the growth of service sector employment in Germany has been slower than in states such as the USA or the UK. In particular, the institutional framework acts as a barrier to the creation of a low-skill, low-wage service economy. There has been little motivation to loosen this constraint as service employment is seen as second rate to industrial employment and because such a 'low road' development (Sabel 1995) is a perceived threat to the stability and equality that the German model promotes. As manufacturing employment has fallen in recent years, Germany has failed to expand service sector employment rapidly enough and this accounts for Germany's persistently high unemployment rates. Instead, policy has sought to reduce rates of economic activity through long periods of education and study, by encouraging early retirement and by not promoting female employment. Alternative strategies need not have been Anglo-Saxon. In the 1980s, the Netherlands tackled the decline of manufacturing employment by promoting part-time jobs, and Sweden encouraged women to take formal employment jobs in the public sector to expand employment levels overall, and quality service sector employment in particular.

Not only does the institutional framework shape the direction of postindustrial transition, it also affects the rate of adaptation. The institutions of the German model were designed to promote consensus and incremental change. The advantage of this approach is that it promotes stability. It avoids the risk-fraught, unstable scenarios that radical transformations bring about. A Thatcher revolution such as in the UK in the 1980s would not be feasible in Germany. This could mean that Germany's transformation is more sustainable in the long run. In the industrial revolution Germany was a late industrialiser and this was seen to be to Germany's advantage. It was able to implement the innovations of early industrialisers, such as the UK or Belgium, in a more efficient way and avoided the risk associated with being pioneers. In a similar way, by taking a delayed and cautious route to postindustrialism, it may be able to avoid the policy mistakes of other more radical transformers such as Britain under Thatcher.

Germany's coexisting postindustrial trajectories

The pattern of strong industrial transformation and weak service sector development is not uniform across Germany and, within this national political economy, there are different regional paths of postindustrial development. To put it another way, unified Germany is characterised by its coexisting postindustrial trajectories. The starting point of this analysis was with Herrigel (1996) who demonstrated that Germany followed different paths of industrialism. These industrial modes and the east German socialist economy were then traced through the ITR (Castells 1996). It becomes clear that postindustrial paths are shaped by their preceding industrial modes and by the regional interpretations of institutional frameworks (Dathe and Schmid 2000: 1). These regional variations of the institutions of the German model are shaping regional variations of Germany's postindustrial transition.

In which directions is Germany developing as a postindustrial economy? As a default starting position it is pertinent to look at the autarkic regions, which were typical of the industrial economy of western Germany. The autarkic industrial region identified by Herrigel (1996) transformed its industrial base what Castells (1996) identified as the Industrial Production Model. The first deviation from this default German norm is the south-west of Germany, which has been exceptionally strong in the way it adapted its industry to new technological developments. Its success in industrial transformation has been attributed to the fact that it is underpinned by the networked or decentralised tradition (Herrigel 1996) which revived in the 1980s and aided the region's economic transition. Additional regional deviations include urban areas, such as Hamburg, which have always had low rates of manufacturing employment and have in recent years developed particularly impressive service economy niches. Other, agglomerated areas, for example around Köln, have also experienced a particularly rapid growth in service sector employment in recent years.

While there are clear regional variations within the western part of Germany, the most significant regional differentiation within Germany concerns the east–west divide. This dimension shows particularly strong deviations form the default German postindustrial path for a number of reasons. The wholesale transfer of the institutional framework of the German model to the east in 1990 clearly shaped east Germany's postindustrial transition. The transfer of the formal institutions to the east was intended to rapidly bring the east up to the industrial standard of the west and to prevent any kind of economic division emerging between the two parts of Germany. However, it has been widely argued that the transfer of the German model to the east in fact had the opposite effect. The currency union and the insistence on the part of trade unions that wages should be equalised as rapidly as possible rendered the east German economy unable to compete and the decline of east Germany's industrial base was accelerated. East Germany was left with no substantial industrial base which could experience technological transformation. What is more, the institutions of the German model, such as industrial relations, training and the innovation systems, have not been properly operationalised or embedded in the east and so, even if there had been much industry left to transform, it is unlikely that the transferred German model would have had the same virtuous effect on manufacturing.

The constraint of the transferred German model also removed any opportunity for eastern Germany to develop along a postindustrial path that was radically different from its west German sponsor. The baggage of the west German model has constrained the east's potential to leapfrog into an alternative postindustrial age, for example, as a low-wage and low-skill economy. Such a development was never going to be tolerated as the concern was that such deviations would undermine the carefully constructed system of the west. That said, there is abundant evidence that the formal institutions of the west are not fully operationalised in the east. This means that there are some distinctively east German postindustrial outcomes which have emerged either out of necessity or out of choice. They might be out of necessity because the economic conditions are not strong enough to sustain the formal institutions; an example would be employers undercutting wage agreements with the agreement of employees. Also, there might be deviations out of choice because the values of the east Germans are different to those in the west. For example, the informal institutions of the east valued industrial employment as a right and duty of both men and women. The desire to work among women in the east remains high today and this challenges the male breadwinner model traditional associated with the west German welfare state.

East Germany's postindustrial trajectories have not yet been clearly forged. While there are isolated examples of industrial success, the east is clearly not an example of the technological transformation of industry familiar from west Germany. It has experienced rapid rates of growth in service sector employment, but there are clear limits to the demand for services in an area of mass unemployment. As an ex-socialist state, it had the potential to leapfrog the east into the postindustrial economy but this possibility was constrained by the rigid framework of the institutions of the German model.

That said, the eastern part of Germany did undergo a rapid process of deindustrialisation and transformation to unstable and precarious postindustrial conditions. What is more, it is possible to identify evidence of the east adapting more rapidly that the west because the institutions are not so rigid and deeply entrenched. There is some evidence that the more weakly institutionalised institutions in the east provide a potential capacity there for faster rates of transformation. This has been seen in the reform of the university system or in more flexible approaches to wage bargaining. There is also evidence of old east German institutions, such as the adult worker model or the reintroduction of childcare and full-day schooling, being reintroduced for the whole of Germany as responses to the challenges of the postindustrial economy. Engler (2002) even goes as far to think of east Germany as a new avant-garde.

East Germany's potential could also be unleashed through opportunities associated with European Union (EU) enlargement to the east. The importance of east Germany will increase after EU enlargement as it is geographically and culturally well placed to become a crucial link between the western and eastern European states. As Thierse (2001) argues, the new *Länder* are the nodal point in a new, enlarged Europe. They could also draw on the experience of old business links to their eastern neighbours which could boost the east German economy. Klein (2002) argues that the interaction during the cold war meant that east Germany and eastern Europe share similar communication cultures which would help business relations.

Hodgson (1999) argues that, learning economies are able to innovate because of the competition that exists between the quirks or impurities in an economic system. The success of Germany as a postindustrial economy depends on its ability to promote postindustrial niches and to allow them to coexist within the single economy rather than expecting a uniformity of performance that formerly characterised the industrial era. Unified Germany is a state which is characterised by a diversity at regional level and each region demonstrates different strengths on its respective path to a postindustrial or learning economy. There is evidence that niches of specialism are being created, or that attempts are now being made to pursue diverse strategies.

If Germany is to maximise the potential of each postindustrial trajectory, it is particularly necessary to allow the east to develop distinct postindustrial niches. Past policies of creating standardised conditions across Germany has been detrimental to the east. As von Dohnanyi (2002) argues, the policies of tax write-offs, investment grants in manufacturing or trying to equalise wages has not helped the east German economy. The theory that lower wages in the east will lead to migration to the west is a myth. It is poor economic prospects and life chances in the east that lead to migration. He argues that an economic location is only attractive to industry if there are opportunities to make a profit. In addition to wage restraint, therefore, east Germany needs regional options for flexibilising all its business regulation. Von Dohnanyi (2002) makes the point that the West German economic miracle in the 1950s would never have happened with the current level of business regulation.

By trying to create a unitary industrial political economy for the whole of Germany after unification, a straitjacket was placed on the east. Had the east been permitted to take a more independent path into the postindustrial economy from the start, unburdened by the rigid and inappropriate institutional framework, then it might not been in the state it is now. In recent years there is growing recognition that the east needs more autonomy to exercise initiative. Significantly, Kurt Biedenkopf, the west German CDU minister president of the east German *Land* Sachsen 1990–2003, conceded in an interview that severe economic mistakes were made following unification. He said, 'we applied west German patterns of thinking on to the eastern regions and, in so doing, partially destroyed them . . . we didn't allow east Germans to develop their own ideas . . . we could have said from the start "go on, have a go" but we didn't' (*Berliner Kurier* 2003: 19).

The crisis of the German model revisited

Much has been written on the strengths and weaknesses of the German political economy in the present stage of capitalism. The crisis has been attributed to it being too highly regulated in the global economy, to the consequences of unification and to the failure of Germany to adapt into a postindustrial economy and society. This book has shown that there is no real evidence either that the German economy is on the verge of collapse or that it is about to converge with other more advanced postindustrial states. Rather, the German economy demonstrates some key strengths in the postindustrial or knowledge economy but also some significant weaknesses. Similarly, it is demonstrating some success in adapting to the new conditions of the new economic era, but there is also some evidence of stickiness. Germany is forging a more cautious trajectory which is determined by its institutional basis and political choices. In a sense Germany is replicating its slow route to industrialisation whereby it developed its industry on the innovations of other industrialised nations such as the UK.

The crisis of the German model is not, then, a failure of the German model to converge to a predetermined postindustrial end state. The crisis is, rather, the consequence of the fact that the German model has not yet adjusted to the demands of the new postindustrial era. One of Germany's main problems in the postindustrial transition is that it has held on to a unitary, industrial framework which was designed for the post-war conditions of West Germany. It has been slow to adapt this institutional framework because it is so well entrenched and because there are interests which seek to preserve the status quo and block efforts to reform practice and alter standards. A further reason for why this unitary and industrial framework has been retained is that unification gave it a renewed legitimacy and lease of life. Despite the fact that discussions about reform of aspects of the German model had been under way in the 1980s, unification entailed wholesale institutional transfer of this model to the new *Länder*. This ossified the model and delayed reform until it was too late. In the post-1945 period the German model sought to create as much unitariness as possible in West Germany and this model was imported on the east at the time of the *Wende* to achieve the same thing. The crisis of the German model is the fact that it is failing to adapt to the diverse conditions of the German postindustrial economy; it effectively acts as a straitjacket.

What is crucial for the future development of the postindustrial Germany, then, is that the German model is reformed so that it is able to respond more rapidly and appropriately to the diversity implied by coexisting postindustrial trajectories. It is imperative that the constraints that hinder the development of certain regions should be adjusted. It is particularly important that the east should be freed up to make the most of its postindustrial advantages. In recent years reforms have been made which aim at modernising the original institutional framework of the German model and these are a step in the right direction. The creation of the trade union ver.di establishes a large-scale union for a diverse service sector; and the reform of codetermination laws makes it easier to form works councils in small and new firms. But a danger nevertheless exists that these will still advantage some regions more than others. For example, ver.di is strong in old areas of service sector such as public services, but weaker in the new areas of economic activity. It is also weaker in the public services in the east and in Berlin, where the public sector employers are on the verge of bankruptcy, they are threatening to leave collective wage agreements. The new laws on codetermination might be appropriate for the established regions experiencing technological transformation of industry, but not in others, where, initially at least, a less regulated approach might be necessary to give business investment a kick-start.

This book concludes that the economy of unified Germany is postindustrial and complex. In order to make the most out of its economy it is necessary for the various postindustrial trajectories to be allowed to coexist with one another in the way that industrial modes coexisted in the past (Herrigel 1996). It will also be necessary to abandon the strategy that persisted in the post-war era of unitary economic conditions and unitary institutional framework in the whole of Germany. Instead, it is vital that regional differentiation in postindustrial development is permitted. This does not mean that the social element of the German model should be abandoned. Rather, social strategies should be sought which are inclusive of all workers, not just the old industrial workers protected by the original framework, and in all areas of the economy. Moreover it should respect the fact that the values entrenched in and perpetuated by the original system do not necessarily match the values of workers such as women or east Germans, for whom the original model was not designed.

Appendix 1
Employment by sector in Germany and its Länder

Germany

	1991 (%)	2000 (%)	Difference
Agriculture, Forestry and Fishery	4.0	2.5	−1.5
Production Industry	36.7	29.4	−7.3
Services	59.2	68.1	+8.9

East Germany including Berlin

	1991 (%)	2000 (%)	Difference
Agriculture, Forestry and Fishery	6.0	3.0	−3.0
Production Industry	37.4	27.2	−10.2
Services	56.7	69.8	+13.1

West Germany including Berlin

	1991 (%)	2000 (%)	Difference
Agriculture, Forestry and Fishery	3.3	2.3	−1.0
Production Industry	36.1	29.3	−6.8
Services	60.6	68.3	+7.7

Appendix 1

Baden-Württemberg

	1991 (%)	2000 (%)	Difference
Agriculture, Forestry and Fishery	3.3	2.2	−1.1
Production Industry	43.0	36.2	−6.8
Services	53.7	61.5	+7.8

Bayern

	1991 (%)	2000 (%)	Difference
Agriculture, Forestry and Fishery	5.5	3.7	−1.8
Production Industry	37.2	31.6	−5.6
Services	57.3	64.7	+7.5

Berlin

	1991 (%)	2000 (%)	Difference
Agriculture, Forestry and Fishery	0.6	0.5	−0.1
Production Industry	28.4	18.7	−9.7
Services	71.0	80.8	+9.8

Brandenburg

	1991 (%)	2000 (%)	Difference
Agriculture, Forestry and Fishery	9.0	4.4	−4.6
Production Industry	36.9	28.4	−8.5
Services	54.0	67.3	+13.3

Bremen

	1991 (%)	2000 (%)	Difference
Agriculture, Forestry and Fishery	0.5	0.5	0
Production Industry	29.4	24.0	−5.4
Services	70.1	75.5	+5.4

Hamburg

	1991 (%)	2000 (%)	Difference
Agriculture, Forestry and Fishery	0.7	0.6	−0.1
Production Industry	22.5	17.5	−5
Services	76.9	82.1	+5.2

Hessen

	1991 (%)	2000 (%)	Difference
Agriculture, Forestry and Fishery	2.5	1.6	−0.9
Production Industry	34.2	26.5	−7.7
Services	63.3	71.9	+8.6

Mecklenburg-Vorpommern

	1991 (%)	2000 (%)	Difference
Agriculture, Forestry and Fishery	11.9	5.1	−6.8
Production Industry	27.4	24.4	−3.0
Services	60.5	70.6	+10.1

Niedersachsen

	1991 (%)	2000 (%)	Difference
Agriculture, Forestry and Fishery	5.4	3.6	−1.8
Production Industry	32.6	27.9	−4.7
Services	62.0	68.5	+6.5

Nordrhein-Westfalen

	1991 (%)	2000 (%)	Difference
Agriculture, Forestry and Fishery	1.9	1.5	−0.4
Production Industry	38.1	29.3	−8.8
Services	59.9	69.2	+9.3

Rheinland-Pfalz

	1991 (%)	2000 (%)	Difference
Agriculture, Forestry and Fishery	4.7	3.0	−1.7
Production Industry	35.3	29.7	−5.6
Services	60.0	67.3	+7.3

Saarland

	1991 (%)	2000 (%)	Difference
Agriculture, Forestry and Fishery	1.2	0.9	−0.2
Production Industry	37.8	31.3	−6.5
Services	61.1	67.8	+6.8

Saschen

	1991 (%)	2000 (%)	Difference
Agriculture, Forestry and Fishery	4.9	2.7	2.2
Production Industry	43.0	31.0	-12
Services	52.0	66.2	+14.2

Saschen-Anhalt

	1991 (%)	2000 (%)	Difference
Agriculture, Forestry and Fishery	7.5	3.8	-3.7
Production Industry	40.7	29.2	-11.5
Services	51.7	67.1	+15.4

Schleswig-Holstein

	1991 (%)	2000 (%)	Difference
Agriculture, Forestry and Fishery	4.8	3.6	-1.2
Production Industry	26.9	23.1	-3.8
Services	68.3	73.4	+5.1

Thüringen

	1991 (%)	2000 (%)	Difference
Agriculture, Forestry and Fishery	6.4	3.4	-3.0
Production Industry	43.1	31.8	-11.3
Services	50.5	64.7	+14.2

Calculations are the author's own.
Source: Statistisches Bundesamt (2001) *Statistisches Jahrbuch 2001 für die Bundesrepublik Deutschland*, Wiesbaden: Statistisches Bundesamt.

Appendix 2

Unemployment in Germany
by Länder (2000–2)

Region	August 2000 (%)	August 2001 (%)	August 2002 (%)
Germany	9.3	9.2	9.6
Total number	3,780,671	3,788,788	4,018,199
Eastern Germany	17.0	17.1	17.7
Western Germany	7.4	7.3	7.8
Baden Württemberg	5.2	5.0	5.5
Bayern	5.0	5.0	5.9
Berlin	15.6	16.1	17.0
Brandenburg	16.4	17.3	17.3
Bremen	12.9	12.5	12.4
Hamburg	8.5	8.1	8.9
Hessen	6.9	6.4	6.8
Mecklenburg-Vorpommern	17.4	17.9	17.9
Niedersachsen	8.9	8.7	8.9
Nordrhein Westfalen	8.8	8.7	9.3
Rheinland Pfalz	6.8	6.6	7.0
Saarland	9.4	8.7	9.0
Sachsen	16.6	17.2	17.7
Sachsen Anhalt	19.9	19.2	19.4
Schleswig-Holstein	8.1	8.2	8.3
Thüringen	14.9	14.9	15.5

Source: Statistisches Bundesamt (2001) *Statistisches Jahrbuch 2001 für die Bundesrepublik Deutschland*, Wiesbaden: Statistisches Bundesamt.

References

Adagh, J. (1991) *Germany and the Germans*, London: Penguin.

Addison, J. T., Bellmann, L., Schnabel, C. and Wagner, J. (2002) *The Long Awaited Reform of the German Works Constitution Act*, IZA Discussion Paper 422, Bonn: IZA.

Ahlers, E. and Dorsch-Schweizer, M. (2001) 'Ver.di und Gender. Die Welt der Betriebe mit hoher Frauenbeschäftigung', *WSI-Mitteilungen*, 12, 759–65.

Albert, M. (1993) *Capitalism Against Capitalism*, London: Whurr.

Amin, A. (1994) *Post-Fordism: A Reader*, London: Sage.

Annesley, C. (1999) 'Postindustrial diversity in unified Germany', in D. Jürgens (ed.), *Mutual Exchanges II*, Frankfurt am Main: Peter Lang.

Annesley, C. (2002) 'Reconfiguring women's social citizenship in Germany: the right to *Sozialhilfe*; the responsibility to work', *German Politics*, 11:1, 81–96.

Annesley, C. (2003a) 'Transforming welfare and gender regimes: evidence from the UK and Germany', *Comparative European Politics*, 1:2, 129–47.

Annesley, C. (2003b) 'Postindustrial challenges to German trade unions', paper presented to PSA labour movements group conference 'Labour Movements Old and New', Salford, 4 July.

Arbeitsamt (2003) www.arbeitsamt.de/hst/services/statistik/english/s001e.pdf (accessed 16 June 2003).

Auer, P. (1997) 'Institutional stability pays: German industrial relations under pressure', in L. Turner (ed.), *Negotiating the New Germany: Can Social Partnership Survive?* New York: Cornell University Press.

Bach, S. and Schupp, J. (2003) 'Beschäftigung im Niedriglohnbereich – Probleme, Lösungsansätze und wirtschaftspolitische Implikationen', *Vierteljahrshefte zur Wirtschaftsforschung*, 72:1, 5–9.

Baethges, M. (2001) 'Abschied vom Industrialismus: Konturen einer neuen gesellschaftlichen Ordnung der Arbeit', in M. Baethge and I. Wilkens (eds), *Die große Hoffnung für das 21. Jahrhundert? Perspektiven und Strategien für die Entwicklung der Dienstleistungsbeschäftigung*, Opladen: Leske und Budrich.

Bahle, T. (2002) 'Eyes and ears wide shut: reform of the university career structure in Germany', *European Political Science*, Summer, 4–11.

Beck, U. (1998) 'Die Seele der Demokratie: wie wir Bürgerarbeit statt Arbeitslosigkeit finanzieren können', *Gewerkschaftliche Monatshefte*, 6–7, 330–4.

Beck, V. (1999) '10 years of female unemployment: an east–west comparison', paper presented at the Past as Prologue? European Transformation and Integration since 1989 conference, Georgetown University, 16–18 October.

Bell, D. (1974) *The Coming of Post-Industrial Society*, London: Heineman.

Bell, D. (1996) *The Cultural Contradictions of Capitalism*, New York: Basic Books.

Berger, R. (1996) 'Standort Deutschland in der Informations- und Wissensgesellschaft', in D. Schulte (ed.), *Arbeit der Zukunft*, Köln: Bund.

Berger, S. and Dore, R. (eds) (1996) *National Diversity and Global Capitalism*, Ithaca, NY, and London: Cornell University Press.

Berliner Kurier (2003) 'Kurt Biedenkopf im Interview', 6 July, 19.

Bertelsmann Stiftung and Hans-Böckler Stiftung (eds) (1998) *Mitbestimmung und neue Unternehmenskulturen – Bilanz und Perspektiven. Empfehlungen der Kommission Mitbestimmung*, Gütersloh: Verlag Bertelsmann Stiftung.

Boden, M. and Miles, I. (eds) (2000) *Services and the Knowledge-Based Economy*, London and New York: Continuum.

Bowley, G. (1998) 'From Jena to Silicon Valley', *Financial Times*, 12 August, 8.

Brint, S. (2001) 'Professionals and the "knowledge economy": rethinking the theory of postindustrial society', *Current Sociology*, 49:4, 101–32.

Bsirske, F. (2001a) 'Ver.di – Aussichten, Chancen, Probleme', *Gewerkschaftliche Monatshefte*, 52: 6, 321–7.

Bsirske, F. (2001b) 'Wegen Umbau geöffnet. Grundsatzrede des Vorsitzenden der Vereinigten Dienstleistungsgewerkschaft ver.di auf dem Gründungskongress ver.di am 20. März', *Die Zeit*, 13, available at www.zeit.de/reden/wirtschaftspolitik/200113_verdi_bsirske (accessed 16 June 2003).

Bulmahn, E. (2002) 'PISA: the consequences for Germany', *OECD Observer*, available at www.oecdobserver.org (accessed 28 June 2002).

Bundesministerium für Bildung und Forschung (BMBF) (2002) *Die deutschen Hochschulen auf dem Weg ins 21. Jahrhundert. An unseren Hochschulen bewegt sich etwas.* Berlin: BMBF.

Bundesanstalt für Arbeit, www.arbeitsamt.de

Campbell, J. (1989) *Joy in Work, German Work: The National Debate*, Princeton, NJ: Princeton University Press.

Castells, M. (1996) *The Rise of Network Society*, Oxford: Blackwell.

Coates, D. (1999) 'Models of capitalism in the new world order: the UK case', *Political Studies*, 47, 643–60.

Coates, D. (2000) *Models of Capitalism: Growth and Stagnation in the Modern Era*, Cambridge: Polity Press.

Czada, R. (2002) 'The German political economy in flux', in J. Leonhard and L. Funk (eds), *Ten Years of German Unification: Transfer, Transformation, Incorporation?* Birmingham: Birmingham University Press.

Czada, R. and Lütz, S. (eds) (2000) *Die politische Konstitution von Märkten*, Wiesbaden: Westdeutscher Verlag.

Darnstädt, T., Koch, J., Mohr, J., Neumann, C. and Wensierski, P. (2001) 'Mangelhaft. Die OECD-Studie Pisa bringt es an den Tag: Im internationalen Vergleich versagen die deutschen Schulen', *Der Spiegel*, 50, 60–75.

Dathe, D. and Schmid, G. (2000) *Determinants of Business and Personal Services: Evidence from West German Regions*, WZB Discussion Paper FS I 00 – 202, Berlin: WZB.

David, P. A. and Foray, D. (2002) 'An introduction to the economy of the knowledge society', *International Social Science Journal*, 171, 9–23.

Deutscher Gewerkschaftsbund (DGB) (1998) *Novellierungsvorschläge des DGB zum Betriebsverfassungsgesetz 1972*, Düsseldorf: DGB.

Doherty, T. (1997) 'Warum die Bundesrepublik Schwierigkeiten mit der neuen Kommunikationswelt hat', *Die Zeit*, 38, available at www.zeit.de/archiv/1997/38/athesen.txt.19970912.xml#top (accessed 16 June 2003).

Dohnanyi, K. von (2002) 'Seit der Einheit schwächelt die Wirtschaft', *Süddeutsche Zeitung*, 5 December, 2.

Edgar, A. and Sedgewick, P. (eds) (1999) *Key Concepts in Cultural Theory*, London: Routledge.

EIROnline (2003) 'Aging crisis looms for Germany', available at www.eiro.eurofound.eu.int/print/2003/06/inbrief/DE030610N.html (accessed September 2003).

Engler, W. (2002) *Die Ostdeutschen als Avantgarde*, Berlin: Aufbau Verlag.

Esping-Andersen, G. (1990) *Three Worlds of Welfare Capitalism*, Cambridge: Polity Press.

Esping-Andersen, G. (1999) *The Social Foundations of Postindustrial Economies*, Oxford: Oxford University Press.

Esping-Andersen, G., Gallie, D., Hemerijck, A. and Myles, J. (2002) *Why We Need a New Welfare State*, Oxford: Oxford University Press.

Esping-Andersen, G. and Regini, M. (eds) (2000) *Why Deregulate Labour Markets?* Oxford: Oxford University Press.

Eurostat (2003) Eurostat News Release STAT/02/101 (29 August 2002) cited in www.ibeurope.com/Database/Resources/R015emp.htm (accessed 25 June 2003).

Fichter, M. (1994) 'Was ist / ist was im Osten los?', *Gewerkschaftliche Monatshefte*, 6, 374–81.

Finetti, M. (2002) 'Ostdeutsche Universitäten an der Spitze', *Süddeutsche Zeitung*, 18 July, 5.

Finke, B., Hornig, F., Jung, A., Kehrer, M., Löhe, F and Werle, K. (2002)'Wir sind die Angeschmierten', *Der Spiegel*, 33, 28–42.

Fourastie, J. (1963) *The Great Hope of the Twentieth Century*.

Fourastié, J. (1969) *Große Hoffnung des 20. Jahrhunderts*, Köln: Bund Verlag.

Frankel, B. (1987) *The Post-Industrial Utopians*, Cambridge: Polity Press.

Fuchs, S. and Schettkat, R. (2000) 'Germany: a regulated flexibility', in G. Esping-Andersen and M. Regini (eds), *Why Deregulate Labour Markets?* Oxford: Oxford University Press.

Fukuyama, F. (1992) *The End of History and the Last Man*, Harmondsworth: Penguin.

Funk, L. (2001) 'Towards a transformed Federal Republic of Germany? Structural change and the renewal of social democratic economic policy', in M. H. Stierle and T. Birringer (eds), *Economics of Transformation: Theory, Experience and EU Enlargement*, Berlin: VWF – Verlag für Wissenschaft und Forschung.

Galbraith, J. K. (1967) *The New Industrial State*, Harmondsworth: Penguin.

Gamble, A. (1985) *Britain in Decline*, 2nd edn, Basingstoke: Macmillan.

Gamble, A. (2000) *Politics and Fate*, Cambridge: Polity Press.

Gerschenkron, A. (1962) *Economic Backwardness in Historical Perspective*, Cambridge, MA: Harvard University Press.

Giddens, A. (1994) *Beyond the Left and Right: The Future of Radical Politics*, Cambridge: Polity Press.

Hall, P. and Soskice, D. (2001) *Varieties of Capitalism: The Institutional Foundations of Comparative Advantage*, Oxford: Oxford University Press.

Hall, P. A. and Taylor, C. R. (1996) 'Political science and the three new institutionalisms', *Political Science*, 46, 936–57.

Hall, S. (1988) 'Brave new world', *Marxism Today*, October, 24–9.

Hamann, G. (2001) 'www.klassenkampf.de', *Die Zeit*, 44, available at www.zeit.de/archiv/2001/44/200144_connex.xml (accessed 25 October 2003).

Harding, R. 91999) '*Standort Deutschland* in the globalising economy: an end to the economic miracle?', *German Politics*, 8:1, 66–88.

Harding, R. and Paterson, W. E. (2000) 'Germany in a global era', in R. Harding and W. E. Paterson (eds), *The Future of the German Economy: An End to the Miracle?* Manchester: Manchester University Press.

Harding, R. and Soskice, D. (2000) 'The end of the innovation economy?', in R. Harding and W. E. Paterson (eds), *The Future of the German Economy: An End to the Miracle?* Manchester: Manchester University Press.

Hartung, K. (1997) 'Überlegungen zum Jahrestag der Einheit: Was der Westen in Osten übersieht', *Die Zeit*, 41.

Hasibether, W. (2001) 'ver.di kommt – Auf dem Weg zur erneuerten Gewerkschaftsbewegung', *Gewerkschaftliche Monatshefte*, 52:3, 172–83.

Häußermann, H. and Siebel, W. (1995) *Dienstleistungsgesellschaften*, Frankfurt am Main: Suhrkamp Verlag.

Held, D., McGrew, A., Goldblatt, D. and Perraton, J. (1999) *Global Transformations: Politics, Economics and Culture*, Cambridge: Polity Press.

Herrigel, G. (1996) *Industrial Construction: The Sources of German Industrial Power*, Cambridge: Cambridge University Press.

Herrigel, G. (1997) 'The limits of German manufacturing flexibility', in L. Turner (ed.), *Negotiating the New Germany: Can Social Partnership Survive?* (New York: Cornell University Press.

Heuser, U. J. and von Randow, G. (1998) 'Was die Ossis besser machen', *Die Zeit*, 8.

Hielscher, A., Koch, J. and Schmidt, C. (2002) 'Uni zum Wohlfühlen', *Der Spiegel*, 30, 56–60.

Hirst, P. and Thompson, G. (1996) *Globalization in Question*, Cambridge: Polity Press.

Hodgson, G. (1999) *Economics and Utopia: Why the Learning Economy is not the End of History*, London: Routledge.

Holm, C. (2002) 'Das bringt uns gar nichts', *Der Spiegel*, 12, 60–4.

Huber, B. (1999) 'IG Metall und Dienstleistungen. Kommt zusammen, was zusammen gehört', *Gewerkschaftliche Monatshefte*, 50:9, 536–44.

Hutton, W. (1996) *The State We're In*, London: Vintage.

Hyman, R. (1996) *Institutional Transfer: Industrial Relations in Eastern Germany*, Working Paper FS I 69 – 305, Berlin: WZB.

Ingelhart, R. (1977) *The Silent Revolution: Changing Values and Political Styles among Western Publics*, Princeton, NJ: Princeton University Press.

International Labour Organisation (ILO) 'Key indicators of the labour market', *World of Work*, 41, December, available at www.ilo.org/public/english/bureau/inf/magazine/41/kilm.htm.

Iversen, T. and Wren, A. (1998) 'Equality, employment, and budgetary restraint: the trilemma of the service economy', *World Politics*, 50:4, 507–46.

Kanzleramt (2001) *Sozialbericht*, available at www.bundeskanzler.de (accessed 13 April 2002).

Keller, B. (1999) 'Neustrukturierung der Interessenvertretung im Dienstleistungsbereich. Eine Gedankenskizze zu ver.di', *Gewerkschaftliche Monatshefte*, 50:10, 609–24.

Keller, B. (2001a) 'Ver.di after the overture: the biggest trade union in the world', *Mitbestimmung*, 7, 20–3.

Keller, B. (2001b) 'Ver.di – oder: Von zukünftigen Schwierigkeiten nach der Euphorie des Zusammenschlusses', *Gewerkschaftliche Monatshefte*, 52:6, 376–87.

Keller, B. (2001c) *Ver.di: Triumphmarsch oder Gefangenenchor?* Hamburg: VSA.

Kenny, M. (1999) 'Marxism and regulation theory', in A. Gamble, D. Marsh and T. Tant (eds), *Marxism and Social Science*, Basingstoke: Macmillan.

Kerr, C., Dunlop, J., Harbinson, F. and Meyers, C. (1973) *Industrialism and Industrial Man*, Harmondsworth: Penguin.

Kitschelt, H., Lange, P., Marks, G. and Stephens, J. D. (eds) (1999) *Continuity and Change in Contemporary Capitalism*, Cambridge: Cambridge University Press.

Kittner, M. (1997) *Arbeits- und Sozialordnung: Ausgewählte und eingeleitete Gesetztexte. 22. Auflage*, Köln: Bund Verlag.

Klein, O. G. (2002) *Ihr könnt uns einfach nicht verstehen. Warum Ost- und Westdeutsche aneinander vorbeireden*, Frankfurt am Main: Eichborn.

Kumar, K. (1996) *From Post-industrial to Post-modern Society*, London: Blackwell.

Kurbjuhn, M. and Fichter, M. (1993) 'Auch im Osten brauchen die Gewerkschaften Gestaltungskompetenz', *Gewerkschaftliche* Monatshefte, 1, 35–45.

Lafontaine, O. and Müller, C. (1998) *Keine Angst vor der Globalisierung: Wohlstand und Arbeit für alle*, Bonn: Dietz Verlag.

Lange, T. and Shackelton, J. R. (1998) *The Political Economy of German Unification*, Oxford: Berghahn Books.

Lash, S. and Urry, J. (1987) *The End of Organized Capitalism*, Cambridge: Polity Press.

Lash, S. and Urry, J. (1994) *Economies of Signs and Space*, Cambridge: Polity Press.

Lepenies, W. (2003) 'Alter Ruhm und neue Armut. Warum Deutschlands Bildungswesen so sehr ins Hintertreffen geraten ist – und wie es den Anschluss wiederfinden könnte', *Psychologie Heute*, January, 60–9.

Lewis, J. (2001a) 'The decline in the male breadwinner model: implications for work and care', *Social Politics*, 8:2, 152–69.

Lewis, J. (2001b) 'Orientations to work and the issue of care', in J. Millar and K. Rowlingson (eds), *Lone Parents, Employment and Social Policy. Cross-national Comparisons*, Bristol: Policy Press.

Mai, H. (1999) 'Der Prozess zu ver.di, der Vereinten Dienstleistungsgewerkschaft', *Gewerkschaftliche Monatshefte*, 50:10, 583–9.

Manow, P. and Seils, E. (2000) 'Adjusting badly. the German welfare state, structural change and the open economy', in F. Scharpf and V. A. Schmidt (eds), *Welfare and Work in the Open Economy. Vol II. Diverse Responses to Common Challenges*, Oxford: Oxford University Press.

Martin, P. and Werner, H. (2000) '"Green Card" für IT-Spezialisten – Was lässt sich aus der Immigrationspolitik der USA lernen?', *Arbeit und Sozialpolitik* 54:9–10, 10–15.

Mattauch, C. (2001) 'Vom Flugblatt zur E-mail', *Die Zeit*, 12, available at www.zeit.de/archiv/2001/12/200112_gewerkschaften.xml (accessed 25 October 2003).

Meyer-Timpe, U., Schäfer, U. and Steingart, G. (2003) 'Abschied von Bismarck', *Der Spiegel*, 11, available at www.spiegel.de/spiegel/0,1518,239603,00.html (accessed 16 June 2003).

Müller, H.-P. (2001) 'Über die Mühen der Profilierung einer Dienstleistungsgewerkschaft', *Industrielle Beziehungen*, 8:1, 108–37.

Müller, P. (2001) 'Ranschmeißen mit halbem Herzen', *Die Zeit*, 33, available at www.zeit.de/archiv/2001/33/200133_gewerkschafttext.xml (accessed 25 October 2003).

Murray, R. (1988) 'Life after Henry (Ford)', *Marxism Today*, October, 8–13.

Murray, R. (1991) 'The state after Henry', *Marxism Today*, May, 22–7.

Nicolai, W. (1998) 'The role of small and medium-sized enterprises in the new federal states', in T. Lange and J. R. Shackelton (eds), *The Political Economy of German Unification*, Oxford: Berghahn Books.

North, D. (1990) *Institutions, Institutional Change and Performance*, New York: Cambridge University Press.

Norten-Standen, G. (1997) 'No history means no baggage', *Guardian*, 6 December.

Organisation for Economic Co-operation and Development (OECD) (1996) 'Germany', in *Social Assistance Regimes in OECD Countries: Country Reports*, Paris: OECD.

Pankoke, E. (1993) 'Work and welfare in Germany: structural crises and the transformation of values in modern industrial society', in M. Pender and M. McGowan (eds), *Work and its Representation in Contemporary German Culture*, Contemporary German Studies Occasional Paper 9, Strathclyde: University of Strathclyde.

Piore, M. and Sabel, C. (1984) *The Second Industrial Divide: Possibilities for Prosperity*, New York: Basic Books.

Pohl, R. (1997) 'Ostdeutschland braucht eine neue Orientierung', *Deutschland Archiv*, 30:3.

Repke, I., Wassermann, A. and Winter, S. (2002) 'Wieder der doofe Rest?' *Der Spiegel*, 3, 42–7.

Rifkin, J. (1996) *The End of Work: The Decline of the Global Labor Force and the Dawn of the Post-market Era*, New York: G. P. Putnam's Sons.

Rifkin, J. (1997) 'Das Informationszcitalter rottet die Arbeit aus', *Die Zeit*, 19.

Sabel, C. F. (1989) 'Flexible specialisation and the re-emergence of regional economies', in P. Q. Hirst and J. Zeitlin (eds), *Reversing Industrial Decline: Industrial Structure and Policy in Britain and her Competitors*, Oxford: Berg.

Sabel, C. F. (1994a) 'Flexible specialisation and regional economies', in A. Amin (ed.), *Post-Fordism: A Reader*, London: Sage.

Sabel, C. F. (1995) 'Bootstrapping reform: rebuilding firms, the welfare state and unions', *Politics and Society*, 23:1, 5–48.

Scharpf, F. and Schmidt, V. A. (2000a) 'Introduction', in F. Scharpf and V. A. Schmidt (eds), *Welfare and Work in the Open Economy. Vol I. From Vulnerability to Competitiveness*, Oxford: Oxford University Press.

Scharpf, F. and Schmidt, V. A. (eds) (2000b) *Welfare and Work in the Open Economy. Vol I. From Vulnerability to Competitiveness*, Oxford: Oxford University Press.

Scharpf, F. and Schmidt, V. A. (eds) (2000c) *Welfare and Work in the Open Economy. Vol II. Diverse Responses to Common Challenges*, Oxford: Oxford University Press.

Scheele, A. (2000) 'Volkswagen presents plans for 5000 new jobs', available at www.eiro.eurofound.ie/2000/03/Feature/DE0003251F.html (accessed 14 June 2003).

Schmid, G. (2003) 'Anpassung an moderne Zeiten. Zur Agenda 2010: mehr Flexibilität und Sicherheit', *WZB Mitteilungen*, 100, June, 7–10.

Schmid, G. and Müller, K-U. (2001) *Die Zukunft der Erwerbsarbeit. Thesen und Perspektiven für Mecklenburg-Vorpommern*, WZB Discussion paper FS I 01–205, Berlin: WZB.

Schmidt, D. (1995) 'Ostdeutschland: Gewerkschaften ohne Solidaritätskultur', *Gewerkschaftliche Monatshefte*, 9, 559–65.

Schmidt, V. A. (1999) 'Convergent pressures, divergent responses. France, Great Britain, and Germany between globalization and Europeanization', in D. Smith, D. J. Solinger and S. C. Topik (eds), *States and Sovereignty in the Global Economy*, London: Routledge.

Schneider, M. (1989) *Kleine Geschichte der Gewerkschaften: Ihre Entwicklung in Deutschland von den Anfängen bis heute*, Bonn: Dietz.

Schröder, G. (2003) 'Training offensive', *Agenda 2010*, available at http://eng.bundesregierung.de/dokumente/Artikel/ix_488146_4317 .htm (accessed June 2003).

Schroeder, W. (2000a) *Industrielle Beziehungen in Ostdeutschland: Zwischen Eigensinn und Paternalismus*, WZB Discussion paper FS III 00–203, Berlin: WZB.

Schroeder, W. (2000b) *Das Modell Deutschland auf dem Prüfstand. Zur Entwicklung der industriellen Beziehungen in Ostdeutschland (1990–2000)*, Wiesbaden: Westdeutscher Verlag.

Schumpeter, J. (1947) *Capitalism, Socialism, and Democracy*, London: Allen and Unwin.

Setterfield, M. (1999) 'Path dependency', in P. H. O'Hara (ed.), *Encyclopedia of Political Economy*, London: Routledge.

Shonfield, A. (1965) *Modern Capitalism: The Changing Balance of Public and Private Power*, Oxford: Oxford University Press.

Siekmeier, F. (1998) 'FDGB als Vorbild? HBV billigt weitere Verhandlungen über Fusion', *Neues Deutschland*, 28 October.

Soskice, D. (1997) 'Stakeholding yes: the German model no', in G. Kelly, D. Kelly and A. Gamble (eds), *Stakeholder Capitalism*, Basingstoke: Macmillan.

Soskice, D. (1999) 'Divergent production regimes: co-ordinated and unco-ordinated market economies in the 1980s and 1990s', in H. Kitschelt, P. Lange, G. Marks and J. D. Stephens (eds), *Continuity and Change in Contemporary Capitalism*, Cambridge: Cambridge University Press.

Spiegel (2002) *Lernen zum Erfolg. Was sich an Schulen und Universitäten ändern muss*, Spiegel special issue 3.

Statistisches Bundesamt (2001) *Statistisches Jahrbuch 2001 für die Bundesrepublik Deutschland*, Wiesbaden: Statistisches Bundesamt.

Steinmueller, W. E. (2002) 'Knowledge-based economies and information and communication technologies', *International Social Science Journal*, 171, 141–53.

Streeck, W. (1997) 'German capitalism: Does it exist? Can it survive?', *New Political Economy*, 2:2, 237–56.

Thelen, K. and Syeinmo, S. (1992) 'Historical institutionalism in comparative politics', in S. Steinmo, K. Thelen and F. Longstreth (eds), *Structuring Politics: Historical Institutionalism in Comparative Analysis*, Cambridge: Cambridge University Press.

Thierse, W. (2001) *Zukunft Ost: Perspektiven für Ostdeutschland in der Mitte Europas*, Berlin: Rowohlt.

Tiemann, H., Schmid, J. and Löbler, F. (1993) 'Gewerkschaften und Sozialdemokratie in den neuen Bundesländern', *Deutschland Archiv*, 26, 40–51.

Timmins, G. (2000) 'Alliance for jobs: labour market policy and industrial relations after the 1998 elections', in R. Harding and W. E. Paterson (eds), *The Future of the German Economy: An End to the Miracle?* Manchester: Manchester University Press.

Viering, J. (2001) 'Korrekturen in letzter Minute', *Süddeutsche Zeitung*, 22 June, 2.

Vitols, S. (2000) 'Globalization: a fundamental change to the German model?', in R. Stubbs and G. R. D. Underhill (eds), *Political Economy and the Changing Global Order*, 2nd edn, Oxford: Oxford University Press.

Voges, W., Jacobs, H. and Tricky, H. (2001) 'Uneven development – local authorities and workfare in Germany', in I. Lødemel and H. Tricky (eds), *'An Offer you Can't Refuse': Workfare in International Perspective*, Bristol: Policy Press.

Wagner, K. (1998) *German Apprenticeship System after Unification*, WZB discussion paper FS I 98 – 302, Berlin: WZB.

Waters, M. (1995) *Globalization*, London: Routledge.

Welsch, J. (2000) 'Green Cards für die New Economy. Eine erste Bilanz', *Blätter für deutsche und internationale Politik*, 45:12, 1473–82.

Wilson, M. (1993) 'The German welfare state: a conservative regime in crisis', in A. Cochrane and J. Clarke (eds), *Comparing Welfare States: Britain in International Context*, London: Sage.

Wirtschaftswoche (2000) 'Brauchen wir eine Green Card für IT-Spezialisten?', *Wirtschaftswoche*, 2 March, 30.

Zohlnhöfer, R. (2003) 'Institutionelle Hemnisse für eine kohärente Wirtschaftspolitik', *Aus Politik und Zeitgeschichte*, B18–19, available at www.bpb.de/publikationen/L3OK3R,0,0,Institutionelle_Hemmnisse _f%FCr_eine_koh%E4rente_Wirtschaftspolitik.html (accessed 1 September 2003).

Zysman, J. (1983) *Governments, Markets and Growth: Financial Systems and the Politics of Industry*, Oxford: Robertson.

Index